STORIES OF
FAITH

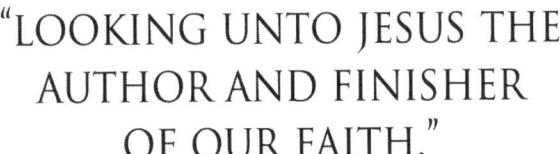

"LOOKING UNTO JESUS THE AUTHOR AND FINISHER OF OUR FAITH."
HEBREWS 12:2

Stories of Faith

Copyright © 2012 Calvary Chapel of Philadelphia

Published by Calvary Chapel of Philadelphia

13500 Philmont Avenue, Philadelphia, PA 19116

E-mail: womensministry@ccphilly.org

ISBN: 978-0-9835950-1-4

All rights reserved. No part of this publication may be reproduced, stored in a retrieval system, or transmitted in any form by any means, electronic, mechanical, photocopy, recording, or otherwise, without the prior permission of the publisher, except as provided by USA copyright law.

First printing for the Women's Seminar, 2012.

All Scripture quotations in this book, unless otherwise indicated, are taken from the New King James Version. Copyright © 1982 by Thomas Nelson, Inc. Used by permission. All rights reserved.

Scripture quotations marked (KJV) are taken from the King James Version of the Bible.

Scripture quotations marked (NASB) are taken from the New American Standard Bible®, Copyright © 1960, 1962, 1963, 1968, 1971, 1972, 1973, 1975, 1977, 1995 by The Lockman Foundation. Used by permission. (www.Lockman.org)

Scripture quotations marked (J.B. Phillips, N.T.) are taken from the J. B. Phillips, The New Testament in Modern English, 1962 edition, published by HarperCollins.

Scripture quotations marked (NIV) are taken from the Holy Bible, New International Version®, NIV®. Copyright © 1973, 1978, 1984, 2011 by Biblica, Inc.™ Used by permission of Zondervan. All rights reserved worldwide. www.zondervan.com. The "NIV" and "New International Version" are trademarks registered in the United States Patent and Trademark Office by Biblica, Inc.™

Scripture quotations marked (TLB) are taken from *The Living Bible* copyright © 1971. Used by permission of Tyndale House Publishers, Inc., Carol Stream, Illinois 60188. All rights reserved.

Cover layout and design: Joanna Liegel

Cover photo: © 2012 Calvary Chapel of Philadelphia

Internal layout and editing: Angie Emma

Internal "shell" photo: ©Thinkstock

Contents

Introduction	1
Preface	3
The Gift of Cancer by Sharon Young	5
Faith that Inspires by Cathy Focht	9
Faith Because He's Faithful by Janie Alfred	17
Faithful in All Things by Joyce Black	19
Power in Jesus' Name by Cheryl Brodersen	24
A Goliath Mission by Debbi Bryson	26
Could This be God's Plan? by Donna Byrd	29
Gently Led by Faith by Angie Emma	33
His Faithful Leading by Hannah Focht	37
Faithful One by Rachel Focht	42
Patient Faith by Sara Gallagher	44
He Is Faithful by June Hesterly	49
My Somewhere Child by Karyn Johnson	51
In His Hand by Jil LaCroix	53
Missing Christopher... *While Living on Promises* by Cathe Laurie	57
My Heavenly Escort by Schylo Lease	62
Believing Faith by Joanna Liegel	70
The Depth of God's Love by Ronnie Lykon	74

Redeeming Faith by Sandy MacIntosh	78
He Who Promised Is Faithful by Jill Martin	84
Never Forsaken by Jean McClure	88
Leap of Faith by Paige McClure	91
An Eternal Hope by Jessica McLean	95
The God of Life by Marisol Morales	97
Beauty from Ashes by Deb O'Brien	103
Under God's Perfect Care by Heidi Paoletti	107
My Rock Through the Storm by Tracy Rios	111
Call to Me by Kay Smith	115
Pray and Believe by Kay Smith	119
Jesus Never Fails by Maude Smith	122
Walk by Faith and Not by Feelings by Kristin Steenbakkers	125
Faith's Expectation by Nancy Sylvester	129
Forever Faithful by Mary Thompson	132
A Walk of Faith Testimony by Carol Wild	137
My Journey of Faith by Evelyn Yerkes	140
Embrace the Race by Pat Zaborowski	145

INTRODUCTION

Calvary Chapel of Philadelphia Women's Ministry put this book together for our 2012 Women's Seminar; the theme of our Seminar was *Faith*. We wanted to give the ladies in attendance a book of *faith* stories written by women who have seen the truth of Hebrews 11:1 worked out in their lives: "Now *faith* is the *substance* of things hoped for, the *evidence* of things not seen."

We want to dedicate these *Stories of Faith* to Jesus, who is "the author and finisher of our faith" (Hebrews 12:2). If it were not for Him coming into our hearts and changing our lives, we would not have these *faith* stories to tell. "For by grace are ye saved through faith; and that not of yourselves, it is the gift of God. Not of works, lest any man should boast" (Ephesians 2:8-9, KJV).

We want to thank Him for all He has done in each of our lives. As you will see in the stories written here, "The things which are impossible with men are possible with God" (Luke 18:27, KJV).

We also want to thank all the ladies who wrote these stories of faith for this book. We are thankful that they were willing to put their hearts on paper for us to be encouraged and inspired…and to see God's faithfulness in such a real way. They are women just like you and me, with faith in an amazing God. They are truly women of faith.

If you do not already know the Lord, we pray that as you read these stories you will be inspired to "have faith in God" (Mark 11:22), because He really is the only one worthy of putting your faith in! "That your faith should not stand in the wisdom of men, but in the power of God." (1 Corinthians 2:5, KJV).

And if you are already a Christian, we hope that after you have read these stories, you will say as the apostles said to Jesus in Luke 17:5, "Lord, increase our faith" (KJV).

"Wherefore seeing we also are compassed about with so great a cloud of witnesses, let us lay aside every weight, and the sin which doth so easily beset us, and let us run with patience the race that is set before us, looking unto Jesus, the author and finisher of our faith; who for the joy that was set before him endured the cross, despising the shame, and is set down at the right hand of the throne of God" (Hebrews 12:1-2, KJV).

May you be blessed as you read this book.

Women's Ministry
Calvary Chapel of Philadelphia

Preface

The first two stories in *Stories of Faith* are in loving memory to our precious sister, Sharon Young. We asked her to write her story because she was such an inspiration to us all! Jesus truly was the "Author and Finisher" of her faith. She wanted her life to give all the glory to God, and it did. Her story is a testimony of an unshakable faith in God. Sharon was the first one that was asked to write a *Faith* story and the first one to finish writing one, so we felt that we should begin the book with her story. She was so excited when we told her that the theme for the 2012 Women's Seminar at Calvary Chapel of Philadelphia was *Faith*. She really wanted to be there, but knew she probably would not live that long.

On September 19, 2011, Sharon, went home to be with the Lord, just two short months after she wrote her testimony. She was 55 years old. We are so thankful that she wrote her *Faith* story and we know it will be an inspiration to all who read it. Sharon truly was a warrior for Jesus!

The Gift of Cancer

Therefore we do not lose heart.
Even though our outward man is perishing, yet
the inward man is being renewed day by day.

2 Corinthians 4:16

I've been a "Christian" for quite awhile now. But I don't think I knew what that meant until I got cancer. Since my very first doctor visit in November 2010, I have considered myself blessed with a gift: an amazing opportunity. Yes, really. Since then, I have not cried once because of the cancer. I have, however, cried many times because of the overwhelming grace of God and the support of so many people that I now know love me!

My original cancer was tonsillar squamous cell carcinoma. Everyone was very upbeat and optimistic about my prognosis. I underwent TORS (TransOral Robotic Surgery) to remove the tumor. Shortly afterwards, I had a neck dissection to remove lymph nodes. Both were successful and I healed well. I went home with a feeding tube for about six weeks, until I could learn to swallow and eat again.

We optimistically thought that all was well. I had a ninety-five percent recovery rate. It was not fun, but the future looked good…until my first routine PET scan a few months later. The scan showed uptakes in my retropharyngeal lymph (behind the throat, in the middle of my head), along with my thyroid, and a few small lesions in my lungs.

So, I had a fine needle biopsy on my thyroid (not fun). Of course, it was inconclusive. Then I went in for a CT-guided needle biopsy of the retropharyngeal (say that five times fast), but when they did the initial scan, lesions on my C7 spine showed up. So they switched gears at the last minute and biopsied my spine at the back of my neck…through my neck (really not fun). Guess what?! That was inconclusive too!

In the meantime, scans were showing that everything was growing very quickly. It was an aggressive cancer. It was also rare to have my particular cancer metastasize the way it did. But…it did. I had to deal with that.

I saw the radiation and chemo oncologists. Chemotherapy was naturally recommended; and they wanted me to enroll in a clinical trial.

Now, my lower back had been hurting for a while, which I attributed to doing yoga. When I mentioned it to the doctor, he ordered three spinal MRIs and a chest CT. A week later another PET scan was performed. The end result of all this scanning and confusion was this: I was given the death sentence of three to six months to live.

I had stage 4 cancer in the middle of my head, my thyroid, all up and down my spine, in my pelvis and my ribs. There were "innumerable" lesions in my lungs. It seemed to me that every time I went to the hospital, it got worse and worse. So, I thought, maybe I should just stop going to the hospital!

We decided to work on my cancer by natural means. I have been blessed with the most wonderful husband I could possibly have. If he has anything to say in this matter…I will get well! I thank and praise God every day for the gift of my husband, John. And I am honored by the love and support of my family and my friends; and happy for the new friends I have made through this time.

What I have found through this adventure is that God is good…ALL the time! All things work for His glory, in His time; and I am willing to be willing. Cancer has given me a tongue and courage, and a fire that I never felt before. It has placed me in situations and circumstances that would not have been part of my life without it. It has given me opportunities to witness and share my testimony and to be a light for the Lord. I pray that I have sown seeds and that He will water them and cause them to grow and reap a bountiful harvest! What a privilege that would be!

The Lord has humbled me. He has broken me. He has refined me. He has awakened me. Most of all, He has given me a holy peace that passes all understanding.

"And the peace of God, which passeth all understanding, shall keep your hearts and minds through Christ Jesus." (Philippians 4:7, KJV).

I have been continuously humbled and overwhelmed with gratitude to my God and the people that I have found out love me! When the pastor and the saints at church pray over me, it brings me to my knees and engulfs me with the power of the Holy Spirit. I cry. Boy, do I cry. I cry tears of joy, knowing that no matter what happens I am in God's hands. And *that* is all that really matters. After all, isn't that our goal as Christians: to stand before the throne and look upon the face of Jesus?

Now of course, being as human as I am, I pray for a miracle. But if I live or if I die…to God be the glory!!! I just pray that I used my gift wisely and that I will hear "Well done, my good and faithful servant" (see Matthew 25:21). Amen.

"Therefore we do not lose heart. Even though our outward man is perishing, yet the inward man is being renewed day by day. For our light affliction, which is but for a moment, is working for us a far more exceeding and eternal weight of glory, while we do not look at the things which are seen, but at the things which are not seen. For the things which are seen are temporary, but the things which are not seen are eternal" (2 Corinthians 4:16-18).

Sharon Young
Calvary Chapel of Philadelphia
July 17, 2011

Faith that Inspires

Looking unto Jesus the author and finisher of our faith.
Hebrews 12:2

I knew Sharon Young for less than a year but her faith will inspire me for the rest of my life. I am so thankful that the Lord allowed us to meet. As I watched her go through her journey with cancer, I saw faith in action in her life. She taught me so much. Hebrews chapter 11 talks about the heroes of faith in the Old Testament and how they walked by faith; to me she was a modern-day woman of faith. Sharon's husband, John, put it perfectly when he would say, "She is my hero." He watched her go through so much and yet be so strong in the Lord.

I met Sharon at a Bible Study we have at our church for women with cancer. Out of the five leaders in the group, three have had breast cancer, one had cancer in the mouth, and I have had skin cancer. The ladies who come have all different types of cancers, but the one thing so many have in common is a relationship with Jesus and amazing courage and faith. What they share out of their suffering is priceless! The faith in this group could easily move a mountain! Jesus said in Matthew 17:20, "If you have faith as a mustard seed, you will say to this mountain, 'Move from here to there,' and it will move; and nothing will be impossible for you." Sharon was one of the ladies that touched all of our lives in this group. She went through her cancer journey with such a sweet spirit and so much faith and grace!

I came to the study one night feeling kind of overwhelmed; I had just been diagnosed with a brain tumor. I was told it was benign (not cancer), which was a relief, but that I would need to see a neurosurgeon every six months for follow up. I was asking the Lord to help me trust Him with this; I didn't want to worry or be afraid about what the future would hold. I wanted to be an encouragement to the ladies that night, but I just felt a little down. Then Sharon walked in. She had two very large scars that went from below her ear all the way down her neck. She had tonsillar squamous cell carcinoma (tonsil cancer) and had two surgeries to remove it. She could barely speak because she was just recovering from the second surgery. She shared with the group that she had cancer. She said,

> *I am not afraid because I know that the Lord is taking care of me, and He has given me such a peace. No matter what happens, I know I am in the Lord's hands.*

I thought that if Sharon could trust the Lord with this serious cancer, I could trust the Lord with a brain tumor. I saw how the Lord was getting her through a much harder circumstance than I was in and it really helped me to trust Him with my situation. God heard my prayer for help to trust Him and He used Sharon! He knows what we need to build our faith in difficult times. It is amazing how He puts people in our path to encourage us! He is the "author and finisher of our faith" (Hebrews 12:2).

As the months went on, Sharon's cancer spread and she got sicker, but her faith got stronger and stronger.

I couldn't wait to come to the Bible study to see her and hear the things the Lord had taught her; she was an absolute joy to be with and such an inspiration to us all. One of her favorite verses was, "I can do all things through Christ who strengthens me" (Philippians 4:13). Sharon knew she could not get through this journey with cancer in her own strength, but she could in His strength.

She really trusted the Lord with her life and what she was going through—that is hard to do sometimes with a serious illness. Psalm 46:1 says, "God is our refuge and strength, a very present help in trouble." He is our help in trouble. We aren't strong, but we have faith in a very strong God. My husband once said, "I don't want to be known as a man of great faith, but as a man with faith in a great God."

Sharon and I became good friends. We prayed for one another, and emailed each other almost every day. We went out to lunch and talked about heaven and how much better it will be there with no more sickness or cancer! She was a heavenly friend! I want to share with you some of the things she told me in her emails that inspired me; they are treasures to me. I pray they will inspire you too.

Sharon was a warrior for Jesus, her courage and faith were amazing. Even when the cancer spread she continued to be an encourager! Imagine getting this email—what faith! She wrote:

The cancer has spread to the retropharynex, thyroid, spine, pelvis, ribs, lungs, trachea, windpipe and lymph nodes. I have a fracture in my lower back. My weight is down to 104 pounds even though I am eating. But praise the Lord that I can still eat at this time. So, as always, prayers are appreciated. And thank you to all my family and friends and brothers and sisters who have been an amazing support and encouragement to me through this adventure! It's been an honor to have you in my life! I continue to pray for God's will and that this cancer not be wasted; that it works to His Glory and can be useful in some way. Nothing goes to waste in God's Kingdom!

"Therefore we do not lose heart. Even though our outward man is perishing, yet the inward man is being renewed day by day" (2 Corinthians 4:16).

She knew that the Lord was with her in every detail of her life, and He could carry her through. She also knew the power of prayer!

The doctor was more somber this time; my percentages are only fifty percent. So, I need to see the oncologists to help me decide about the chemo and radiation. We'll see (lots of prayer on this one).

Please know that I am very comfortable in the Lord's hand, and I know that He will carry me through this. He will give me the strength and the peace of mind to face whatever is coming. I look at it as another opportunity. It's a whole new world and lots of people to meet!

Prayers are always appreciated!

She loved the verse from 2 Corinthians 4:7, "But we have this treasure in earthen vessels, that the excellency of the power may be of God, and not of us" (KJV). She shared this with me:

> *The earthen vessels are perfect! I love that the Lord's light shines through broken vessels! I am telling that to everyone!*
>
> *My PET scan from Friday shows that the cancer is EVERYWHERE basically. My head and throat and neck are full of it. My lungs are jam-packed. It's basically in every bone in my body and my liver. It's just amazing how fast this is happening. But...that just means that the light shines brighter, right?*

She loved that Jesus was the light in her earthen vessel.

She was so thankful to the Lord for His care; even when she had to get a feeding tube she didn't complain:

> *We just got home from the hospital. The feeding tube is in place. God could not have blessed us more today. The day was beautiful. Traffic was excellent. We drove and got down there so quickly I couldn't believe it. Everything went smoothly and in a timely manner. Everyone there could not have been nicer and more caring. One of the nurses was a believer and we had a nice talk with her.*

"For our light affliction, which is but for a moment, is working for us a far more exceeding and eternal weight of glory" (2 Corinthians 4:17). I complain about the smallest things; she taught me that you don't have to do that. She wanted God to be glorified in her life, even through her afflictions—and He was glorified.

She told me she was going to ask the Lord to give her some verses to help her get through this cancer journey. He gave her 2 Corinthians 4:16-18. In verse 18 it says, "While we look not at the things which are seen, but at the things which are not seen: for the things which are seen are temporal; but the things that are not seen are eternal" (KJV). Sharon did see the eternal worth in what she was going through and shared it with everyone. She said this:

> *I love my chemo doctor. She spends hours with us, and she is the most honest and compassionate doctor I have ever been to. I was thrilled that she held hands and prayed with us. I feel that she really feels I don't have long and is looking to make me as comfortable as possible. But like Joe said today... "God is on the throne." So, I wish it was better news, but it is what it is and nothing goes to waste in God's kingdom. Right?*

She loved the Word of God. She said this, *"I'm in the Psalms a lot these days. I'm being put right where I need to be."* Reading His Word gave her the strength she needed each day.

Being thankful was a huge part of Sharon's faith. She thanked the Lord for the good and the bad that she endured. Hebrews 11:27b says, "for he endured as seeing Him who is invisible." Sharon was so thankful for her husband, John, and their daughters, Melissa, Julie and Kristin, and granddaughter, Alexis; they were such a support to her in every way and loved her into heaven. She was an amazing wife, mother, and grandmother. She also was so thankful for her friends and her church. She said:

> *Every single day God is blowing my mind with the love and support that I am getting. I was thrilled*

to make it to church and hear Joe. The music was perfect and it was a blessing to be there soaking it all up and praising Him.

When she couldn't make it to church anymore, she was sad.

I haven't made it to church. I just have no energy. I am just so tired. My weight is down to 98 pounds. I try not to complain, but sometimes it's hard. I hate how cancer takes over your WHOLE life and family…it is so much better in God's world!! I am laying in my bed thinking about CC Philly and being so grateful that the Lord has chosen to allow me to be enveloped in this fold at this time of my life.

I will never forget the day I went to visit her in the hospital during her last hospital stay. She wanted to go for a walk down the hall with her walker. She told me that the doctor had told her she was going to die and that there was nothing else they could do for her. I asked her how she was taking that. She looked at me and said, *"Isn't this what it is all about being a Christian? That we are to look forward to being with Jesus and going to heaven?"* What faith! I said, "Yes, that is right. And we will all be together with Jesus forever, with no sickness or pain." Sharon was living Hebrews 12:2. "Looking unto Jesus, the author and finisher of our faith, who for the joy that was set before Him endured the cross, despising the shame, and has sat down at the right hand of the throne of God." She knew who she had believed! She loved this verse also: "For this God is our God for ever and ever: he will be our guide even unto death" (Psalm 48:14, KJV).

I asked her to write her faith story for us because I was so inspired by her life. A month before she went to be with the Lord, a benefit was put on for her by her employer. We asked her if we could put her faith story in a booklet to give to everyone at the benefit. She said *yes.* Even at the end when she knew she was dying she said, *"My faith has not changed one little bit and never will."* She could say as Paul did in 2 Timothy 4:6-8, "For I am now ready to be offered, and the time of my departure is at hand. I have fought a good fight, I have finished my course, I have kept the faith: Henceforth there is laid up for me a crown of righteousness, which the Lord, the righteous judge, shall give me at that day: and not to me only, but unto all them also that love his appearing" (KJV). She did keep the faith and I pray that her story will encourage those that read it to do the same.

I can't wait to see Sharon again in Heaven. Jesus said, "For God so loved the world, that he gave his only begotten Son, that *whosoever believeth in him* should not perish, but have everlasting life" (John 3:16, KJV).

Cathy Focht
Calvary Chapel of Philadelphia

Faith Because He's Faithful

*This I recall to my mind, therefore I have hope.
The LORD'S lovingkindnesses indeed never cease,
for His compassions never fail. They are new
every morning; great is Your faithfulness.*

Lamentations 3:21-23, NASB

God is so amazing because He tells us that "without faith it is impossible to please God," but He is the one who gives us our initial faith to believe, and continues to increase that faith in our hearts. I believe one way my faith has increased has been through having "stones of remembrance" as I have gone through various trials. I have seen God's faithfulness in my life over and over again.

When I was 13 years old, my parents became missionaries to Brazil. I had never been away from home, and one week after we arrived in the country, my 11-year-old brother and I were sent to a boarding school a thousand miles away from our parents. We had no telephone or other means of communication except through letters that sometimes took up to a month to receive. The theme song for our school was the hymn "Great Is Thy Faithfulness." The theme of that song comes from the verse in Lamentations 3:21-23: "This I recall to my mind, therefore I have hope. The LORD'S lovingkindnesses indeed never cease, for His compassions never fail. They are new every morning; great is Your faithfulness" (NASB).

His faithfulness to me during that difficult time taught me to trust Him in every situation of life. I have learned that God has always been faithful to provide when our finances have been nil; when my children didn't have shoes, and even when my car didn't have hubcaps!! He provided comfort when my parents and sister were killed in a plane crash, and my daughter was killed as a result of her boyfriend's actions.

His faithfulness has given me the ability to have faith and trust in His workings, His plans, and even the trials He has allowed in my life. I have learned that all of it has a purpose: to give me "a future and a hope" (Jeremiah 29:11), as well as to conform me to the image of Jesus (see Romans 8:29). When I remember what He has done, I have faith to keep believing His promises and His faithfulness.

Janie Alfred
Word in Life Ministries
Murrieta, California

Faithful in All Things

*Praise be to the God and Father of our Lord Jesus
Christ, the Father of compassion and the God of
all comfort, who comforts us in all our troubles, so
that we can comfort those in any trouble with the
comfort we ourselves have received from God.*

2 Corinthians 1:3-4, NIV

When I heard the word *cancer* and my name in the same sentence, it felt like my world had stopped. I found a tumor in the back of my mouth in 2004. After a biopsy, I was told that the cancer was called mucoepidermoid carcinoma. It is a rare cancer that is usually found in the salivary glands. The first step was to have surgery to remove the tumor. Since they had to cut such a large section out of the back of my mouth, I needed to have a skin graft. They removed a large portion of skin from my leg to resection it into my mouth. They had to dislocate my jaw to do the surgery. My throat was swollen shut, so they gave me a tracheotomy as a second breathing passage. It was very frightening having the trach. Many times it would start to close up and I would feel like I couldn't breathe, and then I would begin to panic. The Lord stood by my side through it all. He brought His perfect love into my deepest pain to cast out the fear. I wasn't able to swallow, so I had to have a feeding tube. The tube went up my nose and into my stomach. It was very uncomfortable. I don't remember very much of that first week in the hospital except the excruciating pain. It took many months with several set-backs before the pain subsided even a little. Once the swelling in my mouth went down, I was able to have the feeding tube removed; that was such a blessing. I remember sitting in front of the clock waiting until I could take the next pain pill. The medication would only take the edge off of the pain, but it was something. There were days when I didn't think I could go on for even one more hour, but our God is merciful. He taught me to hang on to what I knew to be true and dependable: His unfailing love.

It was during this time that the Lord taught me the power of praise. Through praise we lift our hearts above our troubles and enter God's presence. He inhabits the praises of His people, and I desperately needed His presence. When I praised Him, He filled me with His peace and the knowledge that He was in control.

Anyone who has been through a difficult time asks that initial first question that I found myself asking: *Why me?* But then I realized, *Why not me?* I had always longed to be used by the Lord in whatever way He would choose. In our weakness He shows Himself strong. Physically and emotionally, I felt very weak. This would be an opportunity to let the Lord shine through my pain and uncertainty. "But he said to me, 'My grace is sufficient for you, for my power is made perfect in weakness.' Therefore I will boast all the more gladly about my weaknesses, so that Christ's power may rest on me" (2 Corinthians 12:9, NIV).

The type of cancer that I had has a high recurrence rate. At first they followed up with PET scans every three months, and then every six months. I was always concerned that the test would show that some of the cancer cells had been left behind and had metastasized. I had to make a decision, was I going to allow fear to take over or was I going to trust in the Lord's goodness. I always loved Romans 8:28: "And we know that in all things God works for the good of those who love him, who have been called according to his purpose" (NIV). Now I needed to decide: *Do I really believe this is true? All things—even cancer?* I felt confident He had a plan and a purpose. The Lord brought peace to my heart as I searched His Word. On my darkest days I would cling to Him, choosing to trust Him come what may. I knew that He would use this experience for His honor and glory. I asked for a Scripture to hang onto through this difficult time. He gave me 2 Corinthians 1:3-4 which says, "Praise be to the God and Father of our Lord Jesus Christ, the Father of compassion and the God of all comfort, who comforts us in all our troubles, so that we can comfort those in any trouble with the comfort we ourselves have received from God" (NIV). He began to reveal to me that this time of pain and struggle I was going through would be used for ministry. He was training me during my trial so that I could encourage others who are going through difficult times. I have been cancer-free for eight years now. During those years the Lord has consistently brought people into my life that have cancer, and it has given me an opportunity to tell them of His love and faithfulness.

Before I was diagnosed with cancer, I had been praying that the Lord would give me an open door to share His love with my unsaved family and friends. After my surgery and many follow-up procedures, I was finally able to return to work part-time. Every day people would ask me how I got through it all. They wondered if it had shaken my faith. They would ask, "Where was your God in all this?" I had many opportunities to tell them what the Lord was doing in my life. I was able to share the Gospel with people who never wanted to listen before. That was when I realized that cancer was the answer to my prayer. Cancer opened the door.

I will never know all the reasons why the Lord allowed cancer in my life, but there are many good things that He taught me through it. One of the richest blessings I received from the Lord was that He taught me to get my eyes off this world and the struggles I was going through. When I put my eyes on my Savior and not on my circumstances, He gave me peace, comfort and joy even during my lowest times. When heaven became more real to me, I became less overwhelmed by my situation. The Lord taught me to look to Him and to look forward to that day when He will wipe away all our tears.

Another thing that He taught me was to recall His faithfulness. Through the years I can recall so many times when the Lord has seen me through heartache and pain. He had been faithful before and He would be faithful again. He never changes. The Lord gave me the confidence to trust in His kindness and mercy instead of being overcome by the circumstances.

He has walked with me through these last eight years. I have learned that when the Lord says that He works all things together for the good, He does mean *all* things—even the hard things in our lives. I can look back now and see so many good things that the Lord did for me through my cancer. He strengthened my faith as I watched Him provide for my every need. He sent help and encouragement. He gave me His strength through the pain, uncertainty and fear. He taught me compassion. He showed me that His resources are endless and He supplied what I needed just when I needed it. He gave me a ministry to others who are struggling through cancer.

I don't know what you are going through today, but in a world of uncertainties, I can promise you that if you put your faith in Him, you will not be disappointed. His presence and strength will sustain you. He will carry you through each day. He will never leave you. He will teach you amazing things about His love, His tender care, and His heart for those who are hurting. He can be trusted. You don't have to face life alone. He is all you need.

Joyce Black
Calvary Chapel of Philadelphia

Power in Jesus' Name

*The name of the LORD is a strong tower;
the righteous run to it and are safe.*

Proverbs 18:10

I had been married only two months when I found out I was pregnant. I wanted to share the news with one of my closest friends, Debbie. I called her on the phone and we decided to go get smoothies (a delicious all-fruit drink) from one of our favorite old haunts in Huntington Beach.

After getting our drinks, Debbie and I started crossing the street to my car. As we did, that eerie premonition that something was wrong struck me. I turned around and saw two large, menacing men approaching us. One of the men grabbed my arm on the driver's side of the car. The other man was at the passenger's door and grabbed Debbie's arm.

The man who grabbed me was bearded. He wore denim jeans and a studded leather vest. He was large-framed and wore a leather belt with knife handles protruding out of their sheaths. I began to pray hard. He bent down and in a commanding growl said, "You're going to have a drink and smoke a joint with me!"

Suddenly, as if prompted by the angels of heaven, I began to yell with all my might: "I love Jesus! I love Jesus! I am married, and I am going to have a baby! I love Jesus!"

As I cried out, I heard Debbie begin to yell from the other side of the car: "I love Jesus! I love Jesus! I'm married and I love Jesus!"

The man instantly released his grip on my arm. He looked over the roof of my car and addressed his cohort: "Let's find some other girls. These ones are married."

"Yeah…and they love Jesus," he said mockingly. They turned and walked benignly away from us. We jumped in the car, locked the doors, and began to praise and thank the Lord for His divine protection. We both shared about the power we felt surge through us as we cried out, "I love Jesus!"

That day our faith and confidence in the name of Jesus was strengthened! We both saw the enemy put to flight by the simple declaration of our love for Jesus!

Cheryl Brodersen
Calvary Chapel of Costa Mesa
Santa Ana, California

A Goliath Mission

*Whether you turn to the right or to the left,
your ears will hear a voice behind you,
saying, "This is the way; walk in it."*

Isaiah 30:21, NIV

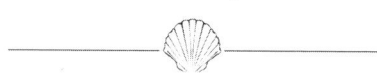

As soon as the iron curtain fell, my husband, George, began to take teams from Calvary Chapels all over the nation into Russia. For 70 years, atheism had been taught in the schools. There was no freedom of religion; Bibles were rare. People were very open—especially in those early years—and eager to receive a Bible and learn more about God. Many Calvary Chapels were birthed at that time. Since then I have taken teams of women to minister at our annual women's conference and visit the orphanages. We have grown to love these women deeply.

Across Russia, women are very vulnerable. There are few opportunities for women from poor families or those coming out of orphanages. These young women are often offered a good job internationally, but it is a scam. Their passports are taken away and they are forced into prostitution. I read an article stating that thousands of Russian women are trafficked into Israel every year; this outraged my heart.

One morning I woke up and clearly knew the Lord had spoken to me. I knew I was supposed to take a team to Tel Aviv, Israel to reach out to the street women. Almost immediately God brought together twenty-two team members who had the same urgency on their hearts. We were a little army of very ordinary, unintimidating-looking women. Trafficking is big money and the people involved are dangerous, but we had weapons that we knew were mighty. We prayed and prayed, and then prayed some more. We had Isaiah 61 printed in English, Hebrew, and Arabic. It says, "the Spirit of the Lord God is upon Me, because the LORD has anointed Me to preach good tidings to the poor...to heal the brokenhearted, to proclaim liberty to the captives...to give them beauty for ashes" (Isaiah 61:1,3). We knew this was the Lord's cause and that He had sent us. We knew His Spirit would go before us like a pillar of fire. We partnered with Calvary Chapel Tel Aviv and did street outreach and a ladies' conference at the church. God miraculously spread the word about the conference to a distant part of the city because our invitations were stolen, and then scattered in the bushes. A little Jewish woman found one on the ground and came. A very large Russian brother escorted and watched over us as we went to the darkest streets to share Jesus with abused and hopeless women. My little army of women wept and ministered, shared testimonies, and led women to Christ. We are still seeing fruit three years later. We stayed at a very low-end Hostel across from the church. People staying at the Hostel accepted Christ too—including one of the workers there.

After our days of ministry, we arranged to have a tour guide take us to see the Holy Land. On the day we were scheduled to go to the Wailing Wall our guide apologized; she had just heard there would be over 6,000 children there.

There had been a severe drought in the land, and the leaders of government had called children from all over the country to come and pray. Immediately I knew we had a divine appointment. With all the problems facing Israel, we had not heard one Jewish person propose prayer as a solution. In response I said, "No, No. This is exciting." I turned to all of our ladies and told them, "We need to pray for these children! Who knows, maybe with the current state of the world, these children could someday be part of the 144,000. They might be the ones who hear the two witnesses preaching here in this very city. No—if the children are coming to pray for rain, we are coming to pray for the children." It was blazing hot that day. The next morning I awoke early. I looked out the window and there was thunder and lightning. I felt like I could see each child press their face to the window and say, "Come look, mom! God answered my prayer." It rained buckets for the next week.

I will share one last miracle of *Goliath* proportion. One of our fervent prayers as a team, along with our prayer partners back home, was against the wicked traffickers themselves. When we arrived home we discovered that the very day we left, the Israeli government made the biggest traffic ring bust in their history. "David said to the Philistine, 'You come against me with sword and spear and javelin, but I come against you in the name of the LORD Almighty, the God of the armies of Israel, whom you have defied" (1 Samuel 17:45, NIV).

Debbi Bryson
Calvary Chapel Church Planting Mission
Biblebusstop.com/Wisdom for Women

Could This Be God's Plan?

*"For I know the plans I have for you," declares
the LORD, "plans to prosper you and not to harm
you, plans to give you hope and a future."*

Jeremiah 29:11, NIV

Faith is always tested when our dreams collide with the Master's plan. Pregnant with our first child, I earnestly prayed God would reveal to me the name for our new baby. Faith stirred within me during worship and my Bible fell open to Jeremiah 1:5: "Before I formed you in the womb I knew you, before you were born I set you apart; I appointed you as a prophet to the nations" (NIV). How exciting to know that we would have a son named Jeremiah, and that he would be ordained by God with a special plan! At that exhilarating moment in time, we could never have imagined the course Jeremiah's life would take. For as the heavens are higher than the earth, so are God's ways higher than our ways, and His thoughts higher than our thoughts (see Isaiah 55:9).

As Jeremiah grew, he proved to be exceptional in many ways. He was blessed with a keen mind and could quickly memorize Scripture. By ninth grade, he had memorized the entire book of Romans, and most of the New Testament epistles. His enthusiasm for learning was rewarded as he was "top of the class" academically, musically and athletically. A natural leader among his peers, he was respected because of his godly character. He was often seen with small groups of children buzzing about him, because of his genuine, fun-loving personality. As parents, we marveled as we watched him grow in "wisdom and stature, and in favor with God and man" (Luke 2:52, NIV). We could hardly wait to see how God would use him for His kingdom.

That fateful summer day, July 13, 1996, our family had made special plans for a fun adventure tubing down the Chattahoochee River with our church's youth group. At one point during the outing, we watched as Jeremiah slid down a waterfall and disappeared into the water. After seconds ticked away, and more seconds, the horrifying reality hit that our fourteen-year-old son was not returning to the water's surface. He was trapped beneath the river's churning waters!

The powerful force of the surrounding rapids prevented us from reaching his submerged body. Minutes passed, yet it seemed like hours, as we desperately cried out to God and to anyone passing by for help. An emergency rescue diver providentially happened upon our situation. After three heroic efforts, he finally delivered Jeremiah's lifeless body from beneath the waterfall where his ankle had been wedged between rocks. The paramedics arrived. Our tearful group joined hands on the sandy shore and pleaded with the Lord to breathe life into his lungs and raise his body from the dead. Hope was waning as he had gone without oxygen for 30 minutes. Then suddenly one of the EMTs exclaimed to our praying circle, "Hey, you guys, keep it up! He is breathing on his own!"

The race for saving Jeremiah's young life stretched into a marathon as he remained in a comatose state. For three long months the Egleston Children's Hospital served as our lifeline, and the Ronald MacDonald House was our temporary home. Throughout all the trauma and uncertainty we faced at the hospital, God's peace was constant. We felt His reassuring presence, experienced His compassion through His people, and received His providential care. We clung to the promises of Scripture believing that God would work all things together for our good (see Romans 8:28). Over and over we received the Jeremiah 29:11 verse in the form of cards, letters, pictures, and gifts. Through those bleak days, God continually reminded us to focus on Him, not on our circumstances, and to trust His promise for a hopeful future for our son.

After arriving home from the hospital, we discovered Jeremiah's journal tucked neatly inside the bookcase in his room. On the date of his accident the recorded scripture reading for that morning was providentially from the book of Job: "But He knows the way that I take; when He has tested me, I shall come forth as gold...for He performs what is appointed for me" (Job 23:10, 14). Like Job, the testing of our faith has been long and full of perplexing trials. Today Jeremiah remains severely brain injured with very limited abilities. He cannot walk or voluntarily move his muscles; therefore, he is confined to a wheelchair and hospital bed. He cannot talk, but communicates joy and sadness through facial expressions. Though now "the world" does not admire his meager accomplishments nor envy his plight, I know Jeremiah has a reward waiting for him in heaven that will far outshine any earthly trophy he could have possibly attained through his previous natural talents.

Most people who are afflicted with such acute disabilities would be relegated to the medical care of a nursing home facility. That was the advice given to us by our doctor when we were discharged from the hospital 16 years ago. By God's grace, we have been blessed to care for him in our home. Along with his three sisters, he is a part of our daily, active family life. Jeremiah is the most contented, joyful person I know. He is extremely appreciative for every kindness shown to him. He often erupts into spontaneous laughter, as if he and the Lord have shared a secret joke.

As the years have passed, we have continued to pray for a miracle. We know that one day when he meets Jesus, Jeremiah will be completely restored. We look forward to the day when we can rejoice in eternity with him and be reunited with our other four children whom we lost to miscarriages. God has a sovereign purpose for every life, no matter how great or small.

I have learned that though the suffering seems unbearable and the expected outcome unacceptable, God will see us through the tough times—and you, too, whatever you are going through. By God's grace, in time, you will eventually adjust to the "new normal," whatever it is in your life. His perfect plan is for us to PRAISE Him everyday for the life He's given, THANK Him for the blessings as well as the challenges, and have FAITH in Him to work all things together for our good and His glory!

Donna Byrd
Calvary Chapel Gwinnett
Buford, Georgia

Gently Led by Faith

*Trust in the LORD with all your heart, and
lean not on your own understanding; in all your ways
acknowledge Him and He shall direct your paths.*

Proverbs 3:5-6

In September of 2009, the Lord allowed me to join my husband on a business trip to Philadelphia. It was my first trip to the East Coast! I was so excited about all the new places and different people I would meet. We had a wonderful weekend of sweet fellowship with new and old friends. Little did I know at that time that the Lord was just beginning an adventure of faith that would lead us to move our family from our home in San Diego, California, all the way across the country to that very place. Looking back I see His hand all along the way, but at the time every step seemed hidden until we stepped out…in faith.

Months passed after our trip to Philly, and we continued on serving the Lord where He had us. But the Lord was stirring my husband's heart that a change was coming; he really felt like God was moving us out…but wasn't quite sure what that meant. We prayed, and then prayed some more. During that time, I found that the greatest place to be was trusting God and not my own understanding. Proverbs 3:5-6 became my daily meditation and took on a whole new meaning: "Trust in the LORD with all your heart, and lean not on your own understanding; in all your ways acknowledge Him and He shall direct your paths." There were things I didn't need to understand or figure out; I just simply needed to trust Him.

Finally, after much prayer we felt that the Lord was leading my husband, Lance, to resign from his job. I was so scared! But I knew that God was leading and that there would be no peace until we obeyed. The crazy thing was that God had only given us clear direction on one thing…the first thing. We didn't know what was next. Looking back I see that our whole journey turned out to be that way. God promised to lead us, and He had been faithful in the past, but He had also asked us to trust Him each step of the way: one step at a time. Many of our friends in San Diego served in the military and they would get new orders every few years as to where they were headed next. Much the same, we got orders from our Commander, but they were sealed orders. We didn't get to see ahead of time where those orders would take us.

During the waiting time, a few different job possibilities were presented to us. One of them would have moved us back to the area where all of our family lived in Orange County, California. So, of course, that was the first place my heart wanted to be. As we prayed, however, God led us in a different direction. Over the course of a few short months, the plans came together for Lance to work for The Joshua Fund and us to move our family to the East Coast. The housing market was not good at the time, so we knew it would take a miracle to sell our house. We were still asking the Lord for wisdom and direction for where exactly He was calling us to live.

During this time of uncertainty and stretching, I studied the life of Abraham. In Genesis 12, God called him to go out of his country to a land he didn't know. God promised to go with him and to bless him. It seemed like God was asking us to do the same. I was encouraged by God's promises that He would never leave us or forsake us, no matter where He led us. We, like Abraham, are "strangers and pilgrims" on this earth, but I had to reconcile in my heart whether I was willing to just say it or really live it.

As we prayed, the Lord kept bringing Philadelphia before our mind's eye; we were drawn to Calvary Chapel of Philadelphia. So we began to step out in faith in that direction. We enrolled our three sons at the school there before our home in California had sold, and waited to see what God would do. Just two weeks before school was to start, our house sold. So the boys and I packed what we could and got on a plane to move to Philadelphia—with one-way tickets. It was more stretching for me because we didn't know for sure where we would live. We believed God was leading us there, and we knew He would continue to be faithful. My wonderful husband stayed behind to handle the details…and pack! But, of course, this meant I was going to a place I didn't know without him for a while. We called it an adventure—and what an adventure it was! I said *goodbye* to my flip-flops and *hello* to a new winter coat. Then I braced myself for living in a hotel for a month with three active, young boys.

Through it all, the Lord was so sweet and faithful to meet our needs, and even exceed them in special ways. We arrived at the airport and were greeted by a new friend that God had brought into our lives a year earlier. She not only met us at the airport that first day, but she stayed with us for our first month here until Lance could join us. What a gift she was to me!

Jesus said, "There is no one who has left house or brothers or sisters or father or mother or wife or children or lands, for My sake and the gospel's, who shall not receive a hundredfold now in this time…and in the age to come, eternal life" (Mark 10:29-30). Truly God has even met that need; not only do we get sweet, fun visits with our family from California, but He has given us a loving new family here in the Body of Christ.

I think the biggest thing I learned through it all, and am still learning, is that God is my loving Shepherd. He knows that I am a sheep who needs to be led. Isaiah 40 says, "He will feed His flock like a shepherd; He will gather the lambs with His arm, and carry them in His bosom, *and gently lead those who are with young*" (Isaiah 40:11). That so encourages my heart! He makes the crooked ways straight, and leads me gently where He desires me to be. Yes, He calls us to live by faith, but He also knows our frame, and will gently lead us step by step—if we will listen to His voice and obey.

Angie Emma
Calvary Chapel of Philadelphia

His Faithful Leading

Thomas, because you have seen Me, you have believed.
Blessed are those who have not seen and yet have believed.
John 20:29

The life of a church kid: that's me. My dad is the senior pastor of Calvary Chapel of Philadelphia. Naturally, church was like my second home growing up—some days spending more hours there than at my own house. I know now that God chose this life for me for His specific plans and purposes, but I didn't always see it that way.

I always told myself that I would be the one in my family who wouldn't end up working at Church—and especially not for the Women's Ministry. I didn't have any good reasoning besides my own pride that viewed a life of serving the Body of Christ as boring and uneventful. All my teenage pride cringed at the idea of planning seminars, picking out decorations, and being around all those women for the rest of my life. I was living in some serious denial to the plans that God had for my life. I would learn how foolish it was to fight the Lord and wear myself out when all He wanted to do was bless me. Pride will do that; it wears us out and keeps us from walking in the blessed paths that God has for our lives.

During my senior year of high school, a few of my friends and I decided that we wanted to go to the Calvary Chapel

Bible College in Murrieta, California. The College is a 2-year program, but my plan was just to go for one year and then go home and start "real college" so that I could get my normal job and live a normal life. In my mind, the purpose of my year at Bible College would just be to gain a solid foundation in my faith in Christ so that I could go home and be strong enough to live for Him, and not fall into the party scene at a secular university. Little did I know how true I would find the Word of God to be in Isaiah 55:8-9 where He says, "'For My thoughts are not your thoughts, nor are your ways My ways,' says the LORD. 'For as the heavens are higher than the earth, so are My ways higher than your ways, and My thoughts than your thoughts.'" God had much different plans in mind for my life than I did, and I would learn to put my faith in Him and His vision instead of trusting in what I could see and what made sense to me.

In August of 2008, my friends and I, and a few of our parents, headed to California—3,000 miles away from home. It was during my time at Bible College that I would find who Jesus really was to me and how sweet it is to have a relationship with the living God. Towards the end of my first year, the Lord continued to put it on my heart to finish the two-year program at Bible College, and drop my plans of going home and starting school there. I remember sitting in one of my classes at the end of that first year and my teacher saying, "Sometimes God is trying to finish a work in your life, but if you're moving around all the time, He can't finish that work. Sometimes you need to stay in the same place so that He can finish that work, even if it's for a year." That pretty much confirmed for me all that God had already been saying, and so in August of 2009, I headed back to California to finish my second year.

It was during my fourth and last semester at school that the Lord really burdened my heart for prayer and how much more I needed it in my life. Among the many things I prayed for that semester, I remember praying and asking the Lord to show me what He wanted me to do after Bible College. With graduation only four months away, the reality of my own uncertainties and lack of understanding in what God had for my life was really starting to hit me. I loved Bible College, had learned so much, and had grown very close to many of the staff members and students. It felt like family and home there, and the thought of leaving was beginning to weigh heavy on me. I was a bit discouraged as well, watching the Lord give many of my close friends clear vision and burdens for ministry or missions, yet I still felt very much in the dark. I remember going to prayer meetings for other countries and the Lord telling me that I could pray but I was not going to go. I was afraid to go back home, though I knew in the back of my mind that was where the Lord was leading me. I was afraid to leave all that I had come to know and love over those two years. I was afraid to leave the people I had gone through so much with and had grown so close to. I was afraid to be uncomfortable and uncertain of the plans that God had for my life. Thankfully, God gave me two close friends who were in similar situations—both feeling the Lord would be leading them home after graduation—and we would pray together. I still had my doubts and just needed to know that I would not be going home out of a lack of faith that

God could lead me somewhere else. Yet again, the Lord sent me undeniable confirmation to put my faith in His leading. I was sitting in my Revelation class, and my teacher said, "If God is calling you to go home, go home." The topic of class that night just so happened to be the Church of Philadelphia! After a short break we walked back into class and my teacher started off by saying, "You know, there is a great sermon by Pastor Joe Focht in Philadelphia…" I couldn't believe what I was hearing! Even after that the Lord continued to confirm to me His plan, whether it was a verse, a phone call from a family member, or randomly running into staff members from my church in Philadelphia on campus!

God was so good to give me all the confirmation that He did in leading me back home, because He knew that I would doubt and that I would struggle with the transition. Whenever doubt did set in, I could look to His Word and His past faithfulness that always brings comfort in present trials. As you may have guessed, *yes,* I do now work for the Women's Ministry at Calvary Chapel of Philadelphia, and I couldn't be more blessed. I finally gave up and realized that God is a whole lot better at planning my life than I am. There is nowhere I would rather be than in the center of His will for my life. Even if it means I can't always see or understand the path that He is leading me on, I can see *Him* and that is all that matters.

During my last semester and in the two years that I have now been home, I sought so much for vision, but learned that sometimes the Lord doesn't choose to give that to us. He wanted me to trust that He knew the plan for my life, and like it says in Daniel 2:22, "He knows what is in the darkness, and light dwells with Him." He gave me so much comfort through those verses that I don't have to worry about knowing what the next step is because God sees my every step from beginning to end, and He will faithfully lead me in the way that I should go as long as my eyes are fixed on Him. Dear Believer, do not be discouraged by or focus on the things that you cannot see, "for we walk by faith, not by sight" (2 Corinthians 5:7). It is a blessed thing to believe the Word of the Lord and His promises without any physical sight or evidence. Just as Jesus says in John 20:29, "Blessed are those who have not seen and yet have believed."

Hannah Focht
Calvary Chapel of Philadelphia

FAITHFUL ONE

*Wait on the Lord; be of good courage,
and He shall strengthen your heart;
Wait, I say, on the Lord!*

Psalm 27:14

"Faith comes by hearing, and hearing by the word of God" (Romans 10:17). Faith is us seeing God for who He is and holding to His character; we learn that by reading the Word. He is good, faithful, kind, patient, merciful, gracious, tender-hearted, and much more.

There have been many times I have needed to rely on God by reminding myself of who He is and by searching the Scriptures that reveal who He is. One instance of this occurred a few years ago. I became pregnant and was extremely excited. I had dreamed of the day that I would become pregnant; I constantly wondered if I would have a little boy or a little girl. I dreamt of what my child would be like as he or she began to talk, and imagined how we would spend our days as he or she grew. When it came time for my first visit I was so excited to go and learn more about my pregnancy. The doctor sent me to get an ultrasound to check to see how the pregnancy was progressing. I couldn't wait to get my ultrasound and see this little one.

However, the pregnancy was not progressing; I had miscarried. When the doctor informed me that I had miscarried I was completely devastated. In the times of my weeping to the Lord, He began to reveal Himself to me in ways that I had never experienced. His Spirit met me when I did not have words to say and when I did not even know what I was thinking. I can clearly recall His presence being with me during the hard days. I felt a peace in the midst of sorrow. He showed me that He truly was my Comforter; the only one with whom I could truly share the depths of my heartache. He alone knew how I was feeling and had the words of truth to share in the midst of this trial. He was patient with me as I questioned Him and His plan. He was kind and gentle, and tenderly comforted my heart over the weeks after my miscarriage.

In the midst of this He gave me Psalm 27:14 to hold onto, "Wait on the LORD: be of good courage, and he shall strengthen thine heart: wait, I say, on the LORD" (KJV). I went over this verse again and again each day. Each day of waiting on the Lord looked different—some days I did better than others.

Overall, God continued to graciously show me that He is truly and intimately involved in my life; He is the God who knows the tears that I cry as well as the cries of my heart. He is a God that wraps His arms around His hurting children and draws them into His bosom. I can say that the Lord is good and is worthy to be praised in all things.

Rachel Focht
Calvary Chapel of Philadelphia

Patient Faith

Therefore do not cast away your confidence, which has great reward. For you have need of endurance, so that after you have done the will of God, you may receive the promise.

Hebrews 10:35-36

 As I sat on the plane leaving Manchester Airport my heart felt like it was about to explode. It wasn't just that I was leaving a place that I loved, and people that I loved; it was that it felt as if I was flying away from the promises of God. My semester in York, England was over, and it was time to go home.

 Bible College for me had been a season of great vision. I went to my first semester in Vajta, Hungary, fired up and ready to see what the Lord had for my life. The Lord had showed me before I left home that Hungary was a step towards something the Lord was going to call me to. I had a great expectation that the Lord was going to lead me somewhere unreached and exciting like India, Turkey, or Afghanistan. What shocked me was that it was none of these places that the Lord was leading me to; it was England. England was the last place I expected the Lord to take me. After months of the Lord persistently calling me, I finally heard Him telling me to go there. When I finally went, I saw that it was exactly where He had been directing my heart all along.

I spent part of the summer between my second and third semester of Bible College at Church on the Way in Bradford, England. The Lord would use these weeks to give me a glimpse of the things He had in store for me. I had the opportunity to lead four children to Jesus, minister to many teenagers, and get to know and love the English people. The Lord had rooted my heart in this place in the way that only He can; I knew I couldn't leave. So, I applied to finish the rest of my semesters of Bible College in York. But, as visa problems would have their way, I ended up spending about six months at home before I ended up actually going to York.

I had months to pray about what the Lord had for me in England before I stepped out to go. One of the verses, among many, that the Lord gave me in that season of waiting was Deuteronomy 11:8-9, 12 and 23.

> *Therefore you shall keep every commandment which I command you today, that you may be strong, and go in and possess the land which you cross over to possess, and that you may prolong your days in the land which your Lord swore… a land for which the Lord your God cares…you will dispossess greater and mightier nations than yourselves.*

The only thing the Lord required of me was to, "Give me your all." I really had to face what it meant to be a follower of Jesus Christ. Was I willing to leave my home, my parents, and my best friends to follow where Jesus was taking me? Was I ready to believe that what God had showed me was actually going to come to pass? That somehow, someway, He really was going to bring a great revival to England?

I went to York ready to see the Lord work, and ready to go wherever He wanted to take me. The only place I wasn't ready to go was back home. I had a great semester in York, but nothing really came from it. No doors opened for me to stay, and it's not like I was marrying some amazing British guy. The only opportunity I had was to get on my return flight to Philadelphia. I felt as if everything the Lord had been showing me was coming to nothing, and that all my hopes were dead.

The Lord was taking me into a wilderness, not because of unbelief, but simply because it was His will. When the Israelites failed to enter into the land at Kadesh Barnea it was because of their unbelief. What I couldn't reconcile was why God would take me out of the "promised land" when I had done nothing wrong. I remember spending hours reading about the Israelites not inheriting the land, and when I really started to feel like I was never going to understand, it hit me: Joshua and Caleb had believed, but they still had to wander for 40 years! They weren't wandering because of their unbelief; they were wandering because God had called them to minister to a wilderness people.

Seeing God lead you away from the very promises He gave you can be the hardest thing in the world to face. But that is the thing; they are His promises—not mine! Do we trust God enough with our promises to put them in His hands and walk away? Believing that He who gave the promise is more than able to keep it? This is what God was calling me to do; to believe that if I would trust Him with those promises that were so near and dear to my heart, that I would see that "what He had promised, He was also able to perform" (Romans 4:21).

God wasn't calling me to understand what He was doing; He was calling me to have faith that His way, which seemed so contrary, was actually the way in which I should walk. Like Abraham, my only hope was to keep on hoping though there be no reason for hope (Romans 4:18).

I set my heart to believe that no matter how "contrary to hope" things may seem I would still believe that God is faithful. I have seen so many friends turn away from the Lord because their circumstances have seemed so hopeless. The disappointment of not getting that relationship, or being turned down by that ministry, can send a young excited believer into a season so dark it seems almost consuming. Faith has a way, however, of turning darkness into great light. Since the day that I left England, I have not had a day where God has failed me. He hasn't always done what I wanted Him to do, but He has always been faithful. In the midst of not being able to be where I so wanted to be, I got to spend a year as shift manager at a Starbucks in the middle of a cult town, sharing Jesus with everyone there. I got to spend a year learning Arabic at Philadelphia Community College, testifying of Jesus to every Muslim I could find. And now, I have just finished my first year working under so many amazing believers here at Calvary Chapel of Philadelphia. I thought that leaving my "promised land" was the worst thing that could have happened to me, but it was actually the best thing I could have done. I have found that truly "He turns a wilderness into pools of water, and dry land into watersprings" (Psalm 107:35).

I am still waiting to see God accomplish many of these things, and I am certainly nowhere near the end of my story.

However, one thing I know is that God is faithful, and He is still able to accomplish all that He has purposed from the beginning, before the foundation of the world, in my life and in yours.

"For the vision is yet for an appointed time; but at the end it will speak, and it will not lie. Though it tarries, wait for it; because it will surely come, it will not tarry" (Habakkuk 2:3).

Sara Gallagher
Calvary Chapel of Philadelphia

He Is Faithful

*Now to Him who is able to do exceedingly
abundantly above all that we ask or think,
according to the power that works in us.*

Ephesians 3:20

In the early seventies, Jim and I were baptized with the Holy Spirit and began to read everything we could get our hands on to help us mature in our newfound Spirit-filled walk. We began to read some of the classics of Christian literature from men and women like Amy Carmichael, David Livingstone, C.T. Studd and George Muller. They all made an impact on us, but one stood out from the rest: George Muller. He fed and cared for thousands of orphans in England simply by faith, never telling anyone when they had a need. He would begin to pray for God to supply, and miracles would happen. This impressed us so much that we made a commitment to live our lives by the same principle of trusting God alone for our support and never asking others for help unless they asked us. An amazing thing began to happen: we began to experience all kinds of financial losses and difficulties. God was testing our faith and teaching us to trust in Him alone.

Many times we had no food to feed our children, but each time as we prayed God would supply. At one particular time we had nothing but a soup bone to put in our pot for soup. As we cried out to the Lord, I remember asking Him for at least some veggies to put with the bone. That afternoon I answered our door bell to find our neighbor standing there with a large bag of meat. She had cleaned out her freezer and had too much for her family to use. Later during the day I went to the mailbox to find a five dollar bill dropped in with the bills. Not only had He supplied meat, but He also supplied for the veggies.

I have to be honest about our life of faith and admit that my husband has far more faith than I have had, and truthfully it has not been an easy road. The enemy always seems to test our commitments to the Lord, but God is the One Who is faithful and cannot fail. He has proven Himself over and over again. He has taken us to numerous countries around the world to share the gospel when we had absolutely no money. He has healed us of our infirmities. He has rescued our prodigal children from the grip of the enemy. He has given us a beautiful home, family, friends, and a place to serve Him. He has been faithful in our youth, in our middle age, and now in our old age. We plan to continue this life trusting in the faithfulness of God until we take our last breath. Ephesians 3:20 has been my life verse. It says: "Now to Him who is able to do exceedingly abundantly above all that we ask or think, according to the power that works in us." He is able.

June Hesterly
Acts 1:8 Ministries
Murrieta, California

My Somewhere Child

*Now faith is the substance of things hoped
for, the evidence of things not seen.*
Hebrews 11:1, KJV

As a foolish young teen I got pregnant! Unable to support her, and too young to parent, I chose adoption for my sweet little daughter. I named her Natalie, which means "the gift of Christmas." Her name was so appropriate because she was born around Christmastime. I believed by faith that someday I would hold her and tell her I loved her, and have the opportunity to share Christ with her. I gave her up with a kiss and a heartfelt promise to find her someday…my somewhere child.

I had a friend who lost an arm in Vietnam. He could still "feel" the phantom pain in that arm. I knew that pain. Every time I felt it I would pray and believe by faith that God would perfect that which concerned me (see Psalm 138:8).

What is faith? "Now faith means putting our full confidence in the things we hope for, it means being certain of things we cannot see" (Hebrews 11:1, J.B. Phillips N.T.).

In my mind, I could see the Master Carpenter working in His "Faith Workshop." My faith and prayers sent Him the wood, nails, glue and screws He was using to build my heart's desire (see Psalm 37:4). My tears were the sand paper He used to round out the rough edges, blowing away the leftover dust of my broken dreams and shattered youth.

Then…one day it happened! Her adoptive mom called me at work! I had given my phone number to the adoption agency I worked with in case they ever wanted it. Her daughter—*my* daughter—wanted to meet me! They named her Linda which means *beautiful* in Spanish. I already knew that! Her mother and father listened to my husband, Jeff, everyday on the radio not knowing he was married to Linda's birthmother. Linda was raised in a Christian home! Even before I placed her for adoption, God knew where to take this baby just like He did with Moses floating down the Nile River and straight into Pharaoh's daughter's arms. A few months after we met I gave her 18 birthday cards, one for each year of her life. I had saved them every year in my "hope chest" for her.

"Faith is the substance of things hoped for, the evidence of things not seen" (Hebrews 11:1). A substance is real! It has form, and so does faith.

To this day, Linda is a "gift of Christmas." She is so very beautiful. It has been 27 years since the day I met Linda and greeted her with her favorite flowers, and a homemade cabbage-patch doll with blue eyes and big, braided pigtails. I still remember when we embraced! Yes, she was real… she WAS the substance of things hoped for, the EVIDENCE of things not seen for 18 years.

God is faithful. He is the restorer of broken branches. What are you sending God to work with in His Faith Workshop?

Karyn Johnson
Calvary Chapel Downey
Downey, California

In His Hand

*My flesh and my heart fail; but God is the
strength of my heart and my portion forever.*

Psalm 73:26

In the fall of 1999, I realized that the lump in my right breast was not going away. I was 37 years old, a stay-at-home-mom, homeschooling our three children—hoping and praying it would just go away. My husband had lost his mom at a young age to breast cancer, so he encouraged me to see my doctor. At the appointment, the doctor felt the lump also, and recommended a mammogram and an ultrasound. This led to seeing a surgeon who did a needle biopsy of the lump. Many friends and family were praying for favorable results, and in November—the week before Thanksgiving—the needle biopsy came back as benign.

After the Christmas holidays, I went back to see the surgeon because the lump was becoming larger and was painful. The surgeon agreed that it had doubled in size. She wanted to perform a lumpectomy because of where the lump was located in my breast. I was very upset and scared. In the back of my mind I really thought this was a cyst. I told the surgeon I just wanted to pray the lump away before the surgery date. She told me that she believed in God and prayer also, and would be praying—but I still needed a lumpectomy. I was amazed that God sent me to a praying surgeon! My fear began to lift, and I felt that Jesus was right beside me holding my hand. He was taking care of me.

I was full of anxiety and worry as I waited for the results of the lumpectomy. By the grace of God, my faith in Him grew as I waited. He strengthened me through His word, prayer, and the gift of comforters in my life.

Finally, the day came when my husband, Pete, and I went to the surgeon's office for the results. I will never forget that day. Before the appointment, I got on my knees beside my bed, and surrendered my life, my anxieties, and fears to God. In the office, Dr. Barnes sat on the edge of the seat with me; she told me that I had breast cancer. My head started thumping, and a rush of fear swept over my body; tears were burning my eyes. I remember Pete guiding me to a bathroom. I kept splashing cold water on my face saying, "God, please help me! I have to be okay for my children." I felt God's presence and His grace calm me down, and put me back together so we could talk to the doctor. The results were not good. Due to the large amount of breast cancer—and that it was invasive breast cancer—I would need a radical mastectomy.

The radical mastectomy, with removal of all my lymph nodes, took place in March of 2000. Recovery, pain, physical therapy to regain use of my right arm, more tests, oncologists and doctor's visits allowed me more time to wait on the Lord. This was a real change in my routine, and I had time to be still before the Lord, and pray and pour my heart out to Him. I couldn't get enough of His word; because in it was life, encouragement, comfort, love, peace, and everything else my heart needed. I was falling in love with Jesus all over again, and it was sweet; far sweeter than the circumstances I was going through. Through it all, I prayed that God would help me to focus on the unseen rather than the things I could see. One Scripture that really helped me through this time was Psalm 62:11-12a. It says, "One thing God has spoken, two things have I heard: that you, O God, are strong, and that you, O Lord, are loving" (NIV). This Scripture reminds me that God is strong, especially when I am not. He is bigger than what I am facing. He will meet me faithfully where I am, and help me through it. He is loving and is always by my side.

My biggest fear was how I would take care of my family as I recovered from surgery, and went through six months of chemotherapy. Would I get through this and be there for my children? It was the most difficult thing for me to let go of. I really had to trust God and all the promises He had given me. And sure enough, He provided everything! Family and friends, and my church family helped me to care for my family. When Pete couldn't take me to chemo, someone else was there beside me. Delicious meals were delivered to our home for months, along with cards, flowers, devotionals, love and prayers. Our needs were met before we even knew we had them. My children kept up with school, music lessons, and even learned to ski that year. "Blessed be the God and Father of our Lord Jesus Christ, the Father of mercies and God of all comfort, who comforts us in all our tribulation, that we may be able to comfort those who are in any trouble, with the comfort with which we ourselves are comforted by God" (2 Corinthians 1:3-4).

I began to recognize that through this trying time, when my heart was broken, God lovingly put the pieces back together! He was beside me holding my hand through it all. He held me in His victorious right hand. I was not a victim of cancer because God uses all things for His glory. He became the strength of my life—He was my sufficiency. The love, grace, mercy, and kindness He showed to all of us was so personal. My heart was overwhelmed to the point that my mouth couldn't help but overflow with His glory. I needed to share what He had done and could do with everyone I came in contact with. I shared with my oncologist how God was using so many people to help me through this illness. She was amazed, and although I am not sure she ever read any of the devotionals I gave her, she still listened. I shared His goodness in the chemo room with doctors, nurses, and, of course, with the other patients I got to know. Even the delivery man and my mailman got to hear the Good News.

During the most difficult year I have ever traveled, many things changed: on the inside and the outside. The Lord healed me, helped me, guided me and showed me His lovingkindness day after day. And most of all, He—the God of all comfort—has comforted me and continues to comfort me all for His glory! My prayer is that I can be used by Him, and that I can have the privilege to comfort others. "One thing God has spoken, two things have I heard: that you, O God, are strong, and that you, O Lord, are loving" (Psalm 62:11-12, NIV).

Jil LaCroix
Calvary Chapel of Philadelphia

Missing Christopher While Living on Promises

Therefore, having been justified by faith, we have peace with God through our Lord Jesus Christ, through whom also we have access by faith into this grace in which we stand, and rejoice in hope of the glory of God.

And not only that, but we also glory in tribulations, knowing that tribulation produces perseverance; and perseverance, character; and character, hope.

Now hope does not disappoint, because the love of God has been poured out in our hearts by the Holy Spirit who was given to us.

For when we were still without strength, in due time Christ died for the ungodly.

For scarcely for a righteous man will one die; yet perhaps for a good man someone would even dare to die.

But God demonstrates His own love toward us, in that while we were still sinners, Christ died for us.

Romans 5:1-8

It was July 24th, 2008.

The day broke, in the cool morning air. The sun shone brilliantly as a breeze stirred in the camphor trees that line the streets of our neighborhood. It was shaping up to be a perfect day; the kind of day on which young moms take their children to the beach, and grandmothers love to remember.

I woke early, made the bed, changed into my running clothes, and tied on my Nikes. I was headed out for a quick, early run. Life was good. Our firstborn son had a beautiful wife who knew Jesus as her Savior, and in the past year even her mother had come to faith. I was happy.

I looked forward to Thursdays when my daughter-in-law, Brittany, and her mom, Sheryll, would come over for a time of Bible study. "Papa" Greg would take Stella for lunch so we could pray and read together. It was good.

Our "perfect day" would last for only a few measured minutes longer, as we were about to face a tragedy that would break in like a cruel thief.

We had been studying through the book of Philippians. That morning the verse I'd set for our time together would be Paul's famous passionate statement in chapter 3, verse 10. "That I may know Him and the power of His resurrection, and the fellowship of His sufferings, being conformed to His death." Little did we realize we would have a crash course on the subject. Only this time, I would no longer be guiding the discussion…He would.

My son was 33 years old. Somewhere on the 91 Freeway between Green River and Serfas Club Drive, Christopher's life on earth would end. He had a daughter who was to celebrate her second birthday in four days, and another baby girl due in four months. Her party would be cancelled, and for many months time would stand still.

It felt like God had taken a big eraser and cleaned the chalkboard of my dreams. He would draw a different picture than the one I had in mind. The colors would be darker and more somber, the lines less straight and crisp. Thomas Merton is said to have written, "God draws straight with crooked lines." It's true.

It is unimaginable planning your son's memorial service, choosing a coffin, a gravesite, an inscription; unimaginable standing in the delivery room watching the birth of his second child without him there. Every holiday, anniversary, birthday, parts of me have been broken—and broken again.

We have never suffered more, cried more, trusted more, or grown more. Getting up in the morning and going to bed at night required strength we didn't have, and only God could give. And He did.

You may have heard people who suffer say things like, "It feels like a punch in the stomach." I can tell you the emotional pain you face one second after you wake knocks the wind out of you. My first thoughts are, *Christopher is gone. It isn't a bad dream. Oh God, help.*

The pain hasn't gone away; it's changed. Trauma over time hurts differently, unfolding and morphing unexpectedly. I stopped asking, "Why?" because I knew that even if I heard the answer, it would be too big for me to wrap my mind around. "How unsearchable his judgments, and his paths beyond tracing out!" (Romans 11:33, NIV).

I do know the Bible is full of stories that helped me; stories of those who could teach me how to live in pain. I suggest you learn them and take notes. They flooded my mind and instructed my heart that dark day.

In the book of Acts, we read the story of how Simon Peter was released from prison; but in the same chapter, the Apostle James was beheaded. Hebrews 11 is full of contrasts. Some women received back their dead, raised to life. Some stopped the mouths of lions, while others were tortured, put to death by stoning. None of us know how our lives or the lives of those we love will play out.

But I can say God is good. I have heard the Lord Jesus' calming voice and felt His nearness. I can stand beside Mary, His mother, at the foot of the cross and hear His cry, "My God, My God, why…?" (Matthew 27:46). I can imagine the tears our Lord, too, has tasted at the tomb of His friend, Lazarus, as he prayed and sweat blood, and cried alone in the garden of Gethsemane. I have a God who suffered. And for that reason, He is my greatest Comforter. He knows what I feel and far, far more. He is able to give me strength I need every day. For this I love Him more.

Just days after the Lord took Christopher home, we received a card from Warren Wiersbe that I keep in my journal. I read it again today on the eve of Christopher's anniversary.

> *Dear Greg and Cathe,*
>
> *As God's children we live on promises, not explanations; and you know the promises as well as we do. When we arrive in heaven we will hear the explanations, accept them, and say, "May the Lord be glorified."*
>
> *Meanwhile, we continue to walk by faith, asking God to help us comfort others, lest our own tears be wasted.*

Your people will detect a new tone in your ministries, whether you sense it or not, and the Lord will accomplish unusual things. Trust Him. Betty and I shall be wrapping our arms around you as we pray for you. It takes time to digest grief, so be patient with yourselves and with the Lord. Jesus saves the best wine for last.

It is all true:

We have lived on promises.

We have no tidy explanations.

We have accepted this, and have seen the Lord glorified in unexpected ways.

We have been comforted, and have comforted countless others.

We have not wasted our tears.

There has been a new tone in our ministries.

God has done unusual things.

We continue to trust Him as we *digest* our grief.

Jesus does save the best wine for last.

Until then, I will wait for that day…

I can almost taste it now.

Cathe Laurie
Harvest Ministries
harvest.org

Story taken from: http://www.harvest.org/virtue/cathes-notes.html?p=5806. Rights and ownership by Cathe Laurie, 2011. Used by permission.

My Heavenly Escort

But without faith it is impossible to please Him.
Hebrews 11:6

It was January 30th, and I was flying out of Los Angeles International Airport (LAX) to go back to New Zealand to continue working at Calvary Chapel Bible Institute. My mother was with me to "send me off," and then was going to fly back to Philadelphia. Some people were concerned about her traveling to the west coast because she was recovering from two recent surgeries. The first was the partial removal of her kidney due to a mass that was perceived by doctors to be cancer. Her second operation was a hysterectomy due to other masses that doctors had found. Her two surgeries and our travels fit into a six-week period. The limitations the doctors placed upon her were to "take it easy and not to carry, push, or pull any handbags or luggage that exceeded ten pounds." Those limitations basically meant that I was in charge of transporting the luggage, which included my guitar, my large suitcase, two carry-on suitcases, and a personal item.

It was about 7:00 pm when we arrived at the airport. My flight was scheduled to depart at 10:00 pm, and my mother's flight back to Philadelphia was scheduled to depart at 10:30 pm. Once we arrived, I went to check-in at the Air New Zealand counter, because that is what the airline ticket in my hand told me I was doing. After an hour's wait, I reached the counter. I then was told that because of my layover in Fiji, I would be flying a different airline first, and then connecting to Auckland with Air New Zealand. Of course, that other airline was in a different terminal! My mother and I began to search for a large cart to carry the luggage to the next terminal, which was said to be an 8-minute walk. As I began to walk out the door, I was stopped by a man who worked for the airline. He began shouting at me and accusing me of stealing his cart. As I tried to explain to him my situation—I was in a hurry, my mother was weak and recovering from multiple surgeries, and I had to carry everything—he continued yelling at me. I saw a couple of police officers out of the corner of my eye. As I made eye-contact with one, I hoped that he would come to our aid, but he did not. He just stood and watched. Finally another assistant came and helped me load two smaller carts; unfortunately, my mom had to push one. As I looked back, my mother waved to me signaling for me to begin walking to the next terminal. I begged the Lord to strengthen her and not allow any of her stitches or incisions to open.

When we finally arrived at the next terminal, my wait to the check-in counter was another hour's worth. I told my mother she should probably go check-in for her flight, which we found out was yet another terminal away. We hugged, prayed, and she departed. She had another hour and a half until her flight was to leave, which I figured was enough for her to walk slowly, check-in, and go through security. I, on the other hand, had about an hour until I was scheduled to depart.

When I finally made it to my terminal, there was a small snack kiosk nearby, so I went to get a bottle of Ginger Ale. I always get sick on planes, and generally can never rest so I was depending on that soda to quell my stomach before I boarded the plane, knowing it was going to be a long and uncomfortable flight. When I went to pay for the drink I realized my wallet was missing. I tried to stay calm as I searched my bag, guitar case, and carry-on for it, but it was nowhere to be found.

When my mom called to see how I was doing I told her of the situation, and like any mother does well, she began to panic slightly. She asked the attendant at her gate if she could leave her bank card for me, but the attendant refused and said it was against their policy. She asked if she should skip her flight so she could come and give me her bank card, but I told her to stay on her flight, praying that I would find my wallet before I left.

I found an airport security attendant and told him my situation; he told me that I needed to go back through and maybe out of security to ask if anyone had found it. Then the next security officer told me to go back to the check-in counters to ask if anyone had found my wallet there. I ran all the way back to the first terminal and asked, but no one had. I then went back to the second check-in counter, and while waiting to speak to an attendant, the handle on my guitar case broke off. The attendant there told me no one had found a wallet. She instructed me to talk with the police to file a missing item report. Putting my backpack on, trying to wedge the slim part of my guitar case between my arm and side, and using the other arm to pull my carry-on suitcase, I set out to find a police officer.

Generally, I hate it when my flight gets delayed, but on this occasion I was thankful that my flight was pushed back two hours. I found a couple of police officers and began to tell them what had happened. They sent out a message on the radio to the officers and the security attendants in LAX with details of what my wallet looked like and where I had last had it. Then another officer came to fill out a missing item report for me. As I began telling her the contents (my driver's license ID, credit cards, bank card, social security card, and a Starbuck's gift card with money still on it), I began to feel sick wondering how everything was going to work out, and praying no one would steal the contents, money...or my identity.

With my missing item report all filled out I began to walk back towards the security gate to return to my gate. From behind me I heard my name being called; it was one of the officers that had helped me. He put $60 in my hand along with his business card. He told me to get something to eat, and try to relax. He and I had talked earlier and I told him I was on my way to go work at a Bible College; he told me he went to a Bible college when he was younger. I thanked him for the money and his kindness and continued on my way.

As I sat waiting for my flight I decided to read Spurgeon's *Check Book of Faith*[1] for that day. Before I opened it up I asked the Lord for it to be something very comforting for me; He answered that prayer. That day's entry reads as follows:

And, behold, I am with thee, and will keep thee in all places whither thou goest. (Genesis 28:15)

Do we need journeying mercies? Here are choice ones—God's presence and preservation. In all places we need both of these, and in all places we shall have them if we go at the call of duty, and not merely according to our own fancy. Why should we look upon removal to another country as a sorrowful necessity when it is laid upon us by the divine will? In all lands the believer is equally a pilgrim and a stranger; and yet in every region the Lord is His dwelling place, even as He has been to His saints in all generations. We may miss the protection of an earthly monarch, but when God says, "I will keep thee," we are in no real danger. This is a blessed passport for a traveler and a heavenly escort for an emigrant.

Jacob had never left his father's room before; he had been a mother's boy and not an adventurer like his brother. Yet he went abroad, and God went with him. He had little luggage and no attendants; yet no prince ever journeyed with a nobler bodyguard. Even while he slept in the open field, angels watched over him, and the Lord God spoke to him. If the Lord bids us go, let us say with our Lord Jesus, "Arise, let us go hence."

As I read it I laughed to myself and thought of how little is my faith, and yet how Sovereign is my God. I apologized to the Lord for stressing out and not trusting Him. Another hour and a half passed before we started boarding the plane. I checked my guitar in at the gate and found my seat next to an older couple. We finally took off around 2:00 am. As I mentioned earlier, I always get sick on planes and can never rest; on this flight, I slept the whole way to Fiji except for meals. It was probably the best, most relaxing flight I have ever experienced. I woke up when we landed in Fiji, and the older couple next to me jokingly calling me "Sleeping Beauty."

Once I exited the plane I had to go check-in for my next flight. I found one of the luggage attendants from my flight and inquired about my guitar case. He hadn't seen it, but told me they would find it. As I went through their security system and found my gate, I waited to board the next plane. As I was boarding, I asked if anyone had found my guitar—no one had. The flight from Fiji to New Zealand is about two hours. I spent most of that time journaling, reading, and asking God to take care of all of my luggage and my wallet.

After two hours had passed, we landed in Auckland. I went to the luggage carousel in hopes of finding my guitar along with my suitcase. However, I found nothing—not my guitar, not even my suitcase. One of the luggage assistants asked me what I was looking for; I told him the description of my belongings. He told me that all of the luggage had already been taken off the plane, so now I would have to go and file a missing item report—my second missing item report of the day! I made my way over to the luggage services counter and began filling out yet another missing item report. After about twenty minutes had passed I heard my name being called over the loud speaker. I told the man at the counter that my name was being called. He came out from behind the counter and went to go find out what was going on. After a few minutes had passed, the service man had not yet returned, but the luggage attendant from the luggage carousel started walking towards me.

"Your name is Schylo Lease right?" He asked.

"Yes," I replied.

"I was calling your name on the loud speaker because I found your wallet by itself just going around on the luggage carousel. Were you missing it?"

"Yes! I lost it at LAX where I filed a missing item report for it. I just started filling out another missing item report for my luggage though."

"Oh, don't worry. My friend from the service counter is fetching it for you." And from behind him, I saw the man from the desk carrying my luggage towards me. Being overjoyed at what had happened and what was currently taking place, I asked the luggage assistant if I could give him a hug, but before he even gave me an answer my arms were around him thanking him.

The next task ahead of me was getting through the biohazard line which at times can take a few hours to go through. I asked the attendants if I would be able to make it through that line and catch my bus that was leaving in an hour and a half. The man from the desk told me I would not get through in time, but after he took care of the next customer, he would come and escort me to the front of the line. However, once I got in line I was not even there for two minutes when a woman in uniform pointed at me and told me to follow her. She escorted me to the front of the line, and within ten minutes I found myself waiting outside at the bus stop.

Although it was a bit of a bumpy journey, it was one where I definitely saw the traveling mercies spoken of in that devotional from Charles Spurgeon. The Lord used this scenario to establish my faith even more, reminding me to trust Him and to have faith in the One who is Sovereign and in control; for "without faith it is impossible to please Him" (Hebrews 11:6).

God bless you all, and may we all grow in faith.

Schylo Lease
Calvary Chapel Bible Institute
Rotorua, New Zealand

---

1. Excerpt taken from *The Cheque Book of the Bank of Faith* by C.H. Spurgeon, published by Christian Focus Publications, Fearn, Ross-shire, Scotland. www.christianfocus.com.

Believing Faith

Jesus said to him, "Thomas, because you have seen Me, you have believed. Blessed are those who have not seen and yet have believed."

John 20:29

My husband and I got married in April of 2006. In June of the same year I found out I was pregnant with twins! I had a bit of a rough pregnancy and the twins were born slightly premature at 34 weeks. They were fine, but had a brief stay in the NICU. One night, as I stood in the NICU with my dad and my husband, my father said, "These two are going to teach you more about the character of God than anything else in your life." I didn't know then how true that would be.

I have always been very independent and stubborn, wanting to do things on my own. So the Lord gave me boy-girl fraternal twins, and sixteen months later another little girl! As our twins grew, I began to notice that our son seemed to be really struggling. I talked to my husband and he thought maybe I was just worrying too much. I still felt like something could be wrong. I sat reading my Bible one morning; the Lord spoke to my heart and asked me if I was willing to give Him my 3-year-old son and my plans for his life. Afraid of what that might mean, I said *no*. After that, things around our house got a bit crazy. I felt like because of my answer to the Lord, everything that could go wrong did.

As I continued to struggle through whether or not I was willing to change my answer to *yes,* the Lord began to break me. How could I say *no* to His will when He had given His Son to die in my place? So, I said *yes* to what the Lord had asked of me…and thought I meant it. Shortly after, my husband began to have the same concerns that I did. We spoke with our pediatrician, and he didn't really have any answers for us. It seemed like every door we tried to open was being shut. We decided just to pray and wait for the Lord to give us an answer; this was not easy. Not knowing how to help my son was the most awful, helpless feeling and would continue for a year. At this point my husband and I were at our wits' end. We felt like we didn't know how to be good parents to our son. We felt like nothing we tried would ease his frustrations. I had been sharing our concerns with one of my close friends who had experienced similar trials. She called me one day and told me that her son's occupational therapist (OT) had offered to talk to me on the phone for free! I called the therapist and she said the words we were longing to hear, "I think I can help your son." Needless to say, we made an appointment.

Through all of this we met another couple at church, Jim and Nicole, that had been working for years with the same OT we were waiting to see. Nicole offered to come with us to our first appointment and we were so thankful. We went to the OT and she did have answers for us. She told us we would have to come every other week and that she did not take our insurance. I went home and called the insurance company and was told they would not pay for my son's treatment. My heart sank. I began to wonder what we would do. Our son needed this, but how would we be able to do it? As I talked to my husband that night through tears asking how could we possibly afford this, he said, "we just need to pray." I knew he was right. Up to this point everything we tried to do on our own had failed. We really felt that the Lord had led us to this treatment and if this is what He wanted for our son, He would provide. That night we prayed together. The next day my husband called me from work and told me that his boss had decided to leave the company. This meant more responsibility and a raise! Not just a raise, but a raise for the exact amount that we needed to pay for our son's therapy! So we began to go every other week to see the OT. While our son was making improvements there was still a struggle.

During all of this the Lord began to bless and grow our friendship with Jim and Nicole. They have four kids. Their oldest son, Edwin, is autistic, and rarely speaks verbally. He looks like a normal 12-year-old boy on the outside, but on the inside he has a deep relationship with the Lord that is way beyond his years. He has a board with letters on it that he uses to spell out what he wants to say and his mom helps him deliver the message that he feels the Lord has given to him.

My dad had been telling our family "Edwin stories" for a few years and I had always wanted to meet him. Our family was at his house one night, and Nicole had been telling me that Edwin had a message for me. After we had been there for a while she said, "Edwin do you want to talk to your friend, Joanna?" He said *yes,* and ran to get his board. As he sat between his mother and me, he began by telling me, "I can tell that you have a deep faith just like your dad." I was thinking,

Yeah right! Not me! He told me that he was praying for me. He went on to say, "You can do lots of things well, but maybe you cannot do all of them right now. The Lord wants you to know that He loves you. You do have faith, but you need to believe." His mom looked at him and said, "You just told her that she had faith, she does believe, are you sure that is what you wanted to say?" As I sat fighting back tears, I told her that I knew exactly what he was saying to me. I knew the things that I had been holding onto, trying to fix in my own power for the past two years. I did have faith, but I needed to believe that the Lord loved my son more than I did; that He knew him better. I needed to believe that He made him and had a plan for him much greater than anything I could ever plan for him or hope for him. I had only said *yes* to the Lord with half of my heart and I needed to let go.

The Lord had to bring me to a boy that cannot talk, who has overcome a struggle much greater than my son's, to tell me to have faith and to believe! The Lord's ways are high above our ways. The best place to rest is in His faithfulness, believing in His promises.

Joanna Liegel
Calvary Chapel of Philadelphia

The Depth of God's Love

We are more than conquerors through Him who loved us.

Romans 8:37

Nothing will ever be able to separate us from the love of God demonstrated by our Lord Jesus Christ when He died for us.

Romans 8:39, TLB

If someone told me that my daughter, Lindsay, would have Leukemia one day I would have never believed them. *Why would God allow my child to have Leukemia?* I had believed that no hardship would come my way. This previous statement is in no way founded on any biblical truth. God *does* allow and use circumstances we never thought could or would happen in our lives for our good, because He loves us and desires to conform us into His image. Lindsay belonged to the Lord. Like Abraham—not even withholding his promised son from God—I had to let go, give up control, and abandon myself to His will. *Could I? Would I?* She was the Lord's, and He loved her more than I ever could. I was learning that no matter how painful the circumstance, the best place to be is in the will of God.

In 1994, my mother went home to Heaven after eight years of battling cancer. God reminded me of His promise in Hebrews 13:5 that says, "I will never leave you nor forsake you." How faithful and true is God's Word! He has never left me, nor has He forsaken me. Every step of the way He has carried me. When I could not see, He assured me He was right there beside me and He knew the way. Little did I know how precious this Scripture would be to me a second time when my daughter, Lindsay, was diagnosed with Leukemia in 1997 at the age of four. This was the hardest path I have walked so far. There were days so painful, so full of grief, I did not think I could make it. On this path God would show me, in a deeper and greater way, His Love.

In the book of Job, he says, "I have heard of You by the hearing of the ear, but now my eye sees You" (Job 42:5). Even though I did not know the outcome of Lindsay's treatment, I felt the reassurance that no matter what, God loved me. His sovereignty and power overwhelmed me. I could trust Him even though I could not *see* the outcome; He knew the end results. Live or die, Lindsay was *His!*

God did not heal my daughter physically, but He did take her safely home to Heaven. Living for Him is what matters! Those questions…those *whys,* and *what-ifs* stole my peace and hope. I read this quote in the beginning of Lindsay's treatment: "Knowing Him is better than knowing why."[1] The more I know Him (Jesus), the more I realize the *whys* are not important. He has proven His love for me at Calvary's cross. He paid my sin debt. He loves me. I titled the story about this time in my life, "The Depth of God's Love," because truly, "we are more than conquerors through Him who loved us" (Romans 8:37b) and "nothing will ever be able to separate us from the love of God demonstrated by our Lord Jesus Christ when He died for us" (Romans 8:39b, TLB). In the loss of my daughter I did not want to go on; I did not think I could go on. But even the physical death and loss of Lindsay could not separate me from God's love. The cross continued to shout, "I love you!" In my hopelessness there was hope—Jesus! I knew God loved me. The truth of His love was holding me and keeping me. His love was and is the anchor of my soul. God's love is the solid rock on which I stand, because all other ground is sinking sand. "There is no pit so deep that he is not deeper still."[2]

> *Who shall separate us from the love of Christ? Shall tribulation, or distress, or persecution, or famine, or nakedness, or peril, or sword? As it is written: "For Your sake we are killed all day long; We are accounted as sheep for the slaughter." Yet in all these things we are more than conquerors through Him who loved us. For I am persuaded that neither death nor life, nor angels nor principalities nor powers, nor things present nor things to come, nor height nor depth, nor any other created thing, shall be able to separate us from the love of God which is in Christ Jesus our Lord (Romans 8:35-39).*

Jesus has conquered sin and death! I will *see* Lindsay again! Jesus has all the answers. Knowing that He loves me assures me that I can trust Him, even when I do not understand or know *why*.

Great is God's faithfulness!

Lindsay's favorite Bible verse was Luke 10:27. It says, "Thou shalt love the Lord thy God with all thy heart, and with all thy soul, and with all thy strength, and with all thy mind; and thy neighbour as thyself" (KJV).

I hope you know Jesus loves you! May we love Him with all our heart, soul, strength, and mind.

Ronnie Lykon
Calvary Chapel of Philadelphia

1. *Tell Me Why,* by Michael Card, © 1999, p. 3. Published by Crossway, a publishing ministry of Good News Publishers, Wheaton, IL 60187. www.crossway.org.
2. *Corrie ten Boom: Her Story,* by Corrie ten Boom, p.159. ©1971. Published by Chosen Books.

Redeeming Faith

Behold, I make all things new.
Revelation 21:5

I walked back into the house and thought, *Where am I? What has happened to my life? What has happened to my dreams? What has happened to my plans? I have no future. I have no hope.* I was too ashamed to tell my family or friends how serious the situation in my marriage had become. *How did I get here?*

If you had asked me about my future when I was a young woman, I could have told you where I was going and what I wanted. Raised in an all-American family, my hopes and dreams were to be a wife and a mother. I wanted to love and be loved. My goals were good and I was about the business of pursuing them. At the age of 20 I moved to California to continue my education, and everything was going as planned. And then, one beautiful spring day, my life took a turn I had never expected. I met a boy named Mike MacIntosh. Unlike me, Mike had not grown up with the privileges and advantages I had enjoyed. He had no plan. He didn't know where he was going and he didn't care. He didn't even know where he had been. But he was handsome, charming and funny and I was captivated by him and convinced that I was going to be his salvation. I really believed that with my love, my background, my education, and my family heritage I could make him whole. After a whirlwind three weeks, I found myself walking out of the Justice of the Peace in Las Vegas as Mrs. MacIntosh, not realizing that Mike had fed me an incredible pack of lies.

After a few months of being married and getting settled into our new life, I realized there was much more to this man than I had ever imagined, and trouble worse than I had ever seen. Mike was searching for God and he thought he could find Him by taking drugs. He was so wretched, so lonely, so lost, and so confused about himself and about life that he actually thought he would find meaning in drugs. I had no idea how desperate the situation really was; Mike had been taking mind-altering, mind-destroying drugs and unbeknownst to me had filled our garage with them. When I began to realize how lost he really was, I desperately sought to save our marriage thinking getting a house and having a child would accomplish that. However, things went from bad to worse.

Mike was rarely home, spending most of his time either doing drugs or in the bars, occasionally stumbling home in the middle of the night after the bars closed. Things escalated to the point where a drug-lord attempted to break into our home. After that Mike tried to make things better, becoming very involved in Eastern religion. But all of his efforts failed and things continued to get worse. During one of his late night returns home, I got pregnant. I found myself with a nine-month-old baby and another on the way, no money and an absentee husband. I was quickly coming to the end of myself and began to beg Mike to get it together and become the husband and father that he needed to be. Everything I had planned and hoped for my future had been shattered. I moved back home to Philadelphia and prepared to divorce Mike.

After having our second child and filing for divorce, I attempted to get my life back together. I moved back to California and enrolled in Cal State Long Beach. At the same time as I was working to save my life, Mike's life was becoming more and more desperately destroyed. After overdosing, Mike became a shell of a man and would often show up at my apartment unable to form a coherent sentence or do anything but cry.

In the midst of all of this, I worked on getting my life back on what I felt was the right track. I had no idea that the only thing that could really save my life was faith in Jesus Christ. In fact, Mike would be the first one to realize this.

One day I had a familiar knock on my door. Immediately I could see a difference in Mike. He began to ask me if I knew Jesus Christ. At the beginning I was upset and angry, thinking that Mike was once again just trying another religion. But the most amazing thing began to happen; I saw him begin to get well and real change became evident in his life. I could only wonder, *What is this power that has done what my love was unable to do?* One day Mike called me and asked me to come see for myself the things that he had been talking about. To get him to stop bothering me, I got a babysitter and went to the beach where there was a Christian concert and mass baptism going on. I would realize on this day that life changing faith in Jesus Christ was what I needed and had been searching for all along.

Other than the detour I had made with Mike, I was a woman who made decisions carefully. So it was out of character for me to walk up to this crowd of people and get in line to be baptized. Standing next to me was a big old surfer. He turned to me and said, "Are you going to get baptized?" I said, "I think so." "Are you saved?" he asked. I told him I wasn't sure. "Well, I've been saved now for three weeks so let me lead you in the sinner's prayer," he replied. There was no time to think, no time to question, and no time to figure it out. The line was moving and pretty soon it was going to be my turn. I bowed my head and asked the Lord to forgive my sins and save me. Before I knew it, I was in the water being baptized. When I emerged I was instantly changed and filled with the Holy Spirit. I think God worked this way in my life because if He had given me five minutes to think about it I would have said, "No, thank you. That makes no sense at all. The plan of salvation is totally illogical."

I had finally figured out what I needed. I didn't need a husband or a family. I didn't need to be loved by a man. I didn't need the American Dream. I didn't need an education or a plan. I needed a Savior! And once I had Him, I had everything I needed. I had a best friend. I had a lover of my soul. I had the One who had redeemed me, restored me, released me, renewed me, and captured my heart forever. I was so full of joy and hope. I developed new plans for my life and, though I was enjoying a new friendship with Mike, those plans did not include a romantic relationship with him.

However, as time went on Mike began calling and telling me that he believed the Lord wanted us to get remarried. I was persistent in telling him that I was pretty sure that wasn't God's will and that I was perfectly satisfied and happy as I was.

And then one day as I was driving to class, I found myself having a conversation with the Lord. I was saying, "Lord, You are wonderful. I can't imagine how I ever lived without you. I know that it can't be Your will that I end up with this guy again. Being married to him was so painful." It was a conversation that I had had many times with the Lord, and I had always believed He was in perfect agreement with me, because He was always quiet. But on this day, He did not choose to be quiet. A very deep, authoritative voice spoke a Scripture to me that I did not even know existed. It said, "Behold, I make all things new" (Revelation 21:5). Startled I thought, *Whoa... is my radio on?* I pulled the car off the road, shut off the engine, and checked the radio. I was so new in the Lord, so fresh and eager, that I whispered, "Lord, are you talking to me? Do you actually speak out loud to people?" Again I heard a voice as clear and as authoritative as any I had ever heard in my life. The voice said, "Behold, I make all things new." That was all I needed. I turned the car around, went home, and called Mike. I said, "Ok, you're right again. God wants us to be married."

It took faith to obey the Lord and step into something that before had caused so much pain. But as a result of that act of faith, the Lord blessed me and gave me a renewed love for Mike. I actually found myself excited to step into something I had dreaded for so long. We waited a year to get remarried, and though the wait was hard, it was well worth it.

As I walked out of the church on our wedding day, with our little girl and our two-year-old son, I was in awe of how God had redeemed my life. He is incredibly extravagant in

His love, mercy, and grace, and in His healing and restoration. God had given me a new future, a hope, and a family. All the things I had always wanted were now mine.

Sandy MacIntosh
Horizon Christian Fellowship
San Diego, California

Story taken from *Redeemed & Restored.* © 2005 Sandy MacIntosh. Used by permission.

HE WHO PROMISED IS FAITHFUL

Let us hold fast the confession of our hope without wavering, for He who promised is faithful.
Hebrews 10:23

My father was an old-fashioned man. He was born in 1899 when expressing your feelings was foreign to a man, and talking about the deep things of the heart was unthinkable. Yet I always knew that he loved me and would die for me. He told me one time that if I ever lost my eyesight, he would give me his eyes. I used to ask him to tell me that over and over again as a little girl because somehow it communicated to me his heart—even though being told "I love you" was almost embarrassing for him to say.

I got saved in 1971 and felt a great burden for my unsaved family, especially my father. A year after being saved, I knew God wanted me to go home to live and mend some bridges by repenting before my parents for my rebellious attitudes. I was living in Philadelphia; my family lived in New York where I was raised. I really did not want to go home, but I knew God wanted me to trust Him and move in faith. I knew that He would supply the things I was worried about—a church, Christian friends, and a job. My dad had fought on the Mexican border in 1916, in World War I and II. I had protested the Vietnam War in the late sixties and early seventies, so there was a big chasm between us and probably much sorrow in my father's heart about his daughter. We lived the "generation gap." So home I went to repent of a proud and scornful attitude toward my parents and all that they stood for, and to ask forgiveness for how I had hurt them. But more than that, I wanted to tell them about why I was repenting. It was because I had been totally captured by the love of Jesus Christ; He had changed me. I spoke with them about this amazing love and the way of salvation. They easily forgave me and listened intently to what I told them about Jesus. I figured they were thinking, "Oh, here she goes off again onto something else." I remained in New York for six months. In many ways it was a wilderness experience because I never found a church, and only one Christian friend. Jesus Himself sustained me, and the times of worship and fellowship with Him, while essentially being alone, were times I will always cherish. No one got saved, but seeds were planted, and faith was required of me that Jesus would take care of my parents and their salvation. When I moved back to Philadelphia, I knew I had done what God wanted me to do. He had my church, Christian friends—and even the job I had left—waiting for me. I wrote my dad a 10-page letter telling him how much I loved him and how much Jesus loved him. I mailed it off and it was never mentioned by my father or me. Remember, my father was an old-fashioned man that did not talk about things of the heart. Knowing he was uncomfortable with such things, I left it with God.

Ten years later, my folks moved to Florida to retire. That first year there my dad was diagnosed with cancer. He was operated on in April of 1981, only to have the cancer spread to his brain. One week when I called him on the phone, he could speak, and the next week his speech was gone. He was declining fast, so I knew I had to get down to Florida to be with him. My heart was so heavy—not just because I knew I was losing my dad—but more so because I had never prayed with him (except as the designated person to pray at holidays). I had never heard him confess Jesus as his Savior. I knew he always had a fear and respect of God, but somehow I felt he believed he was too much of a sinner to come near to God because he had divorced before he married my mom—unheard of back in the 1940s.

So I went down to Florida to see him—I knew for the last time—and to talk to him about Jesus. I had everyone praying for me. I went with urgency, faith, and a lot of sorrow. I didn't know how God was going to save my dad now. He couldn't even talk and was pretty much in a coma. How would he ever be able to confess Jesus? My heart was never so burdened. When I got there and went into his bedroom it was one of the hardest things to see—a once strong and commanding man, so frail and so sick. I went to the side of his bed and took his hand. By this time I could hardly see him through the tears. All I could do was ask him, "Daddy, do you love Jesus?" Tears spilled out of his eyes, and he cried and cried. He couldn't do anything—speak or move his head or anything, but he knew it was me and he knew what I said. My heart filled as my eyes spilled over with tears.

That night before falling asleep, God spoke to me. I have not had God speak so clearly to me in my entire life. Though it was not audible, it was as if Jesus sat next to me and spoke.

He said, "I will take care of your father." I needed nothing else but my earthly father's tears and my heavenly Father's promise.

A few months after my father's passing into his heavenly home, I went down to help my mom clean out my dad's things. As I was going through his drawer, I came across an old box where my dad kept his war medals. I opened it up. There, with his precious medals that he valued so much, was the 10-page letter I had sent him ten years earlier. I then knew what that letter confessing my love for him and Jesus' love, meant to him. All I could do was express my great gratitude to my God for His faithfulness to hear the prayer of my heart and to take care of my dad. For I know whom I have believed and am persuaded that He is able keep what I have committed to Him until that Day (see 2 Timothy 1:12).

Jill Martin
Calvary Chapel of Philadelphia

Never Forsaken

*The things which are impossible with
men are possible with God.*

Luke 18:27

I have found that even when my faith is small, it does not hinder God from doing great things. Jesus said it could be the size of a mustard seed and mountains could be moved. It isn't how big my faith is, but how big my God is that makes the difference.

Today I read in *Streams in the Desert,*[1] a quote by George Muller. He lived in the 1800s in England and was a great man of faith. He wrote: "When it seemed impossible for help to come, it did come; for God has His own unlimited resources. In ten thousand different ways, and ten thousand different times, God's help may come to us."

It was many years ago: my husband, Don, and I had gotten married at Christmastime, and graduated from college that following June. We had just met a man named Alan Redpath, a minister from Great Britain. He was a guest speaker at our home church in Pasadena, California. He told Don that we needed to go to Bible school in England (at a place called Capernwray), before he went to Seminary. So that fall, we sold our cars, stored our stuff, and headed for the North of England for nine months. That year changed our lives forever. Besides the inspiring teaching from God's Word, we also learned great practical lessons.

Two of those times stand out vividly in my mind. They both would always remind us that God knows what we need, and He does provide, especially when it looks impossible. During our spring break at Bible school we had one week off. We wanted to go to L'Abri Fellowship in Switzerland. It was another Bible school started by a man named Dr. Francis Schaeffer, tucked up in the gorgeous Alps near Lake Geneva. Needless to say, we were not making any money, and therefore couldn't afford to make the trip; it would take two hundred dollars. I remember praying, "Lord if you want us to go, would you provide the money? You know just what we need." A few days later, two hundred dollars came in the mail. Don's sister had sold a little business we had been in together, and that was our share of what was left. Both the timing and the amount were just perfect. The trip was such a blessing to us. Knowing God provided the funds to go made it one of those great lessons from above.

The second experience was our trip home; we had round trip tickets on a charter flight that we had booked nine months in advance. We flew out of London and landed in Oakland, California. The little plane was so packed with students that it seemed to sag in the air as it was lifting off the ground. I was three months pregnant at the time and not feeling very well; I slept a great deal of the way. But while I slept, Don prayed. He didn't want to worry me, but our plane was landing in Oakland, and we didn't have tickets to get to Southern California, which was home—and nearly 400 hundred miles south of where we were landing. *What were we going to do?* He had exactly $20.00 left in his pocket after nine months at school. No wonder he didn't sleep very well. When we landed in Oakland there were chain link fences that people could wait behind while they watched the passengers disembark from the plane. When we walked off the plane, we looked down and saw Don's precious parents waiting for us. You can imagine how happy we were to see them. They said they hoped we didn't mind that they had driven all the way from Southern California to meet us and drive us home. They thought it would be a nice trip, and they hadn't seen us for so long; they wanted to surprise us. Two people never looked so good! They treated us to a wonderful American hamburger and a nice hotel. How wonderfully God had provided for us that entire year, right down to the lovely ride home. I learned He never forsakes us, and He knows what we need. I don't need a lot of faith, just a little; I have a very big God! That was the beginning of our marriage and our ministry, and He, after all these years, has never failed us once. Luke 18:27 says, "The things which are impossible with men are possible with God." Our God is the God of the impossible.

Jean McClure
Calvary Way Ministries
Corona del Mar, California

---

1. *Streams in the Desert,* by L.B.Cowman. Copyright © 1997 by George Muller. Used by permission of Zondervan. www.zondervan.com

Leap of Faith

Now faith is the substance of things hoped for, the evidence of things not seen.

Hebrews 11:1

As I read Hebrews 11:1, I reflected back to the night when I truly rededicated my heart to Jesus Christ.

Let me start with a little background on my life before I tell you about my leap of faith that changed the course of my whole life.

When I was a little girl, I loved God with all my heart. As I grew up, I drifted away from Him only to get caught up in the nothingness the world had to offer me. I tested and tried everything I could to satisfy the void in my heart that once belonged to the Lord; and nothing, I mean nothing, satisfied me the way He could. Without getting into grave detail, I'll just tell you that I made a lot of poor choices that hurt myself and those I loved. My lifestyle was far from a walk with the Lord. In fact, I considered myself a strong atheist and would make fun of any Christian that crossed my path. After a few years of this lifestyle, I got sick and tired of being sick and tired. I was constantly doing the same thing over and over again expecting different results. I was trying to live in the world and experience peace. I tried this in many different worldly fashions. But like I said before, nothing I did in the world could ever compare with the peace that passes all understanding and the freedom I gained in Christ.

Now, going back to the night I rededicated my heart to the Lord, I was 17 (well…I am still 17, but this was about 9 months ago today), and I had been invited to church by a close friend. The first time I went, I sat in the back and barely paid any attention to the youth leader as he spoke on the love of Christ. Two weeks later, I was sitting at the front, hands held high, praising God. I knew with all my heart that nothing could truly satisfy me except Him. I told Him that night, after two weeks of cautiously testing out the waters at church, and seven years of walking without Him, that my life was now His; He could do with it what He wanted.

At the time I was living in Orlando, Florida. I was in a relationship with a guy, was in college, had a job, a life and friends, and even a cat. I wasn't planning on moving anywhere. So when I told God that He could have my life, I thought that meant maybe I would go to some Christian classes or serve in a ministry near my house. I would live out my walk with Him in the comfort of my surroundings. Well, I was very wrong, because when I told God He could do whatever He wanted with my life—and meant it—that's exactly what He did.

After asking God to take my life and use it, I made a phone call to my grandpa who works in full-time ministry. I asked him if he knew of any Christian schools I could save up for around my neighborhood. He told me he would give me a call back and see what he could do. I didn't expect what happened next. He called me back and asked if I wanted to go to a mission training school in Montana—in just a few short days. He said I didn't need any money, and he would pay for my ticket to get there. As I heard him talk about Potter's Field Ministries, and how I would be dedicating a year of my life to the Lord to grow and serve Him, I couldn't help but think, *This is God! This is what He wants me to do.* As soon as that thought came, another thought came to mind: *This would mean I would have to break up with the guy I'm seeing, drop out of college, quit my job, leave my family and my friends. Did I really want to go learn about God and serve Him with people I had never met and just heard about two minutes ago?*

Without hesitation I said, "I want to go! I want to serve God and tell the world about Him! If this is what it takes, I am in 100 percent." From that conversation, things just fell into place. I talked to Mike Rozell, the founder of Potter's Field Ministries, and a few other pastors that served there. They had room for me to go and study with the class that had started in July. I was on a plane no more than four days later. It took faith for me to tell my family, friends, school, boss, and boyfriend why I was about to get on a plane—in four days—and leave my life behind for 365 days to see what God wanted to do with me.

I have to admit, the plane ride was full of tears and confusion, but the peace that was in my heart knowing that the Lord would take care of me was beyond my understanding. It was the very thing that kept me going and abiding in His will. I now see that the faith I had to take such a huge step into an unknown direction was a gift from God. The next nine months of being a part of the IGNITE Mission Training School at Potter's Field Ranch changed my life completely. God not only restored back to me everything I laid at His feet—a job, a family in Christ, education, friends—but I now have something so much more valuable. I have a relationship and foundation set so deep in Christ that there is no moving me. I came to serve God with 365 days of my life, but now I see this ministry as my home and will be here until God calls me somewhere else. I know that I will be serving Him and living out my life with faith until I look into His eyes and hear Him say, "Well done, my good and faithful servant" (see Matthew 25:23).

Oh...did I mention that I had a great-grandparent praying for me when I wasn't walking with the Lord? She was praying that I would meet someone who would invite me to church—and I did. The power of prayer takes faith, because it accesses God, who is the most faithful of all. His plans were much bigger than me just showing up for church when invited—they were to change my life completely. Amazing, huh? I owe a thank you to Great-grandma Gigi for being faithful in her prayers for me, and to Grandma Mimi, who prayed for me too.

I hope this will be a great encouragement to all grandparents and parents to keep the faith! Our God is a great God. Never stop trusting in the power of prayer that God gave us through His Holy Spirit. I will always be grateful that they prayed for me, and their prayers were answered—even if it took seven years.

Paige McClure
Potter's Field Ministries
Whitefish, Montana

An Eternal Hope

*And God shall wipe away all tears from their eyes;
and there shall be no more death, neither
sorrow, nor crying, neither shall there be any more
pain: for the former things are passed away.*

Revelation 21:4, KJV

Since the day I dedicated my heart and life to Jesus as a teenager, I always trusted in the Scripture, "Now faith is the substance of things hoped for, the evidence of things not seen" (Hebrews 11:1, KJV). However, I never thought I'd have to really learn what this verse truly meant.

I am a big sister and have always been a family girl. I happily took on the big sis role and became a second mom to my two younger brothers. My brother, Josh, and I became very close because we had to overcome so many obstacles together, including abandonment and rejection by our biological father. He and I just understood each other.

In 2006, Josh began a spiraling battle with addiction. We all were devastated because we knew the seriousness of the situation. For six years, we fought the addiction battle face on—my brother most of all. Through multiple rehabs, Teen Challenge, sober living facilities and periods of sobriety, the addiction always reared its evil head. And so began the biggest faith battle of my life.

I had never prayed for something so much—hoped for change with all of my heart—begging, pleading, crying out to God for intervention on my brother's behalf. There were times when God did intervene, and I always gave Him all the glory.

But last year on Valentine's Day, while on a date with my husband, Nic, I received a phone call that changed my life forever. My mom called and told me that Josh had an accidental fatal overdose. My heart was instantly shattered. All of my faith, all of the hope I had clung too, seemed to have let me and my brother down. I felt abandoned by God and struggled for over a year to understand this great loss.

One thing that gave me great peace and comfort was the reality of heaven. I wanted to read every book about the subject because Josh lives there now. It was no longer a concept or fantasy place that I believed I would go to one day. It suddenly became so *real.* This was when I began to see what true faith was. True faith is believing in something we can't see. I can't see heaven, but I truly believe with all of my heart that it is real, and that Josh is there! He is waiting for me, fully surrounded by God's glory and love in a place of perfection and light. Experiencing such loss, I have learned that I have the greatest hope of all. I will see Josh again. And that is what allows me to carry on in faith.

Jessica McLean
Singer/Songwriter
Kitty Hawk, North Carolina

The God of Life

Let us hold fast the confession of our hope without wavering, for He who promised is faithful.

Hebrews 10:23

To me, life has always been a bit challenging, but in my heart I thought I had always been spiritual. So, I knew to count my blessings. At the end of nearly ten years of marriage, my husband and I had a traumatic house fire; I thank God we were not home. That very same year as we bounced around from his parents' home to my parents' home, we found out we were finally going to have a baby. Not the best timing, but when you wait for ten years to have a baby, any timing is good timing. This was a huge blessing!

When our precious little boy was three, we decided it was a good time to try for another baby. That summer and fall we had four miscarriages. The babies only made it six to eight weeks. The first two were very hard to deal with, but by the last two, we were already numb from the heartache. I remember feeling, *How much more can we deal with?*

I had started seeing a fertility specialist between the third and fourth miscarriage, when I discovered a lump in my breast. I had pain for about six months, but thought it had something to do with the pregnancies. Since both his aunt and mother had breast cancer, my husband insisted that I get a mammogram right away. The fertility specialist thought it could be a cyst and suggested that we wait a couple months to see if it would just go away. Just by the expression on my face she decided she would send me for a mammogram if I wasn't able to carry the fourth pregnancy, which I was not.

The mammogram showed a suspicious lump, which lead to a needle core biopsy. The result prompted a phone call to me at work telling me that I had cancer. I felt as though my life was over. I worried that my son would grow up without a mother. *Who would take care of him the way I do?*

Whatever happened, I knew I needed to be strong for my family. I told them I would do whatever it took to fight this thing, but deep in my heart I knew that ultimately it was God's decision. I didn't believe in modern-day miracles. Surviving stage 2B cancer would most likely be something that I wouldn't be entitled to do. I would just have to accept it.

Since the tumor was large, the doctors wanted to try neo-adjuvant therapy (chemotherapy before surgery). They hoped this would shrink the tumor, which would allow the surgeon to take it out completely. If it did not shrink it enough, he would have to go back in to remove more. So the plan was four rounds of chemo, followed by a lumpectomy, then four more rounds of chemo, followed by thirty-three daily radiation treatments.

As cancer treatments started, God started sending His angels. One night, a friend called to see how I was feeling. I explained to her that my heart felt like a little crab had clamped on it and wouldn't let go. Since I knew she was spiritual, I shared with her that I was trying to be okay with the diagnosis. If God wanted me to die then I would have to go without kicking and screaming. She said, "Our God is a healing God, and still heals." I didn't understand what she meant at the time, but now Proverbs 4:20-22 speaks to my heart where the Lord says "My son, pay attention to what I say; listen closely to my words. Do not let them out of your sight, keep them within your heart; for they are *life* to those who find them and *health* to a man's whole body" (NIV).

There was a blizzard on the day the tests and scans were scheduled. We had to follow behind a convoy of salt trucks to make it to the hospital. Ironically, here we were fighting a snow blizzard to get to the hospital to start fighting to stay alive. At the hospital, a nice nurse who was looking over my chart and taking my vitals, stopped and looked at me. She said, "You know you're going to go through a lot." I nodded, "Yes, I know." She told me she would like to pray for me. I agreed, of course, that I could use all the prayers I could get. She went to get my husband, because we were going to go through this together. When he entered the room, we all held hands and bowed our heads. While we were in prayer it was as though I could sense the Lord's heart! He was telling me (not in words, but in a profound feeling, that He is alive!!! …and that He was going to be with me). I felt as though something heavy was being pulled off my shoulders and the little clamped crab feeling let go. As she finished her prayer, I hugged her and shared with them my profound feeling of the Lord's presence. I still didn't understand what all this meant, but I did know that God was very close and would not leave me. I consider what it says in Matthew 18:20: "For where two or three are gathered together in My name, I am there in the midst of them."

After the operation, I received a visit from my cousin. I hadn't allowed any visitors at the time, but she was special. We are close in age, and as teenagers we became very close in spirit. We used to always talk about religion and had fun debating my Catholic upbringing with her Christian upbringing. I loved these conversations because she never made me feel that I was wrong even though what she said made a lot of sense. She said something that day that caught my attention; she told me that God must think that I was a very strong woman. I asked her why she thought that. She said that He has given me a lot to handle, and if He didn't think I was strong enough, He wouldn't have allowed me to go through all this. In remembering her words, I think of 2 Corinthians 12:9, "My grace is sufficient for you, for My strength is made perfect in weakness." I am a strong woman only because in my weakness His strength makes me strong. Before she left, she prayed for me and invited me to her church, which she had done many times before I got cancer. I promised her that when I felt better I would definitely join her.

The day finally came when I was able to accompany her to Calvary Chapel. I was still weak and exhausted from chemo, but it was one of my better days. Pastor Joe was teaching from Isaiah 40:27-31. There were hundreds of people around me, but I felt that the message was just for me; it blew my mind. All the verses spoke to my heart, but especially verses 29-31 where it says, "He gives power to the tired and worn out, and strength to the weak. Even the youths shall be exhausted, and the young men will all give up. But they that wait upon the Lord shall renew their strength. They shall mount up with wings like eagles; they shall run and not be weary; they shall walk and not faint" (TLB). I held onto those verses as I finished up with my cancer treatments. Slowly I returned to work and started attending Calvary Chapel with my husband and son; we all got saved. About a year or so later, I had lunch with my cousin. She told me she prayed for my salvation for fifteen years. Her faith led not only to one person's salvation, but to three.

I have learned priceless lessons during my journey with the Lord; things like unconditional love, trust, true happiness, forgiveness, compassion and much, much more. The Lord continues to work on these lessons with me at deeper levels as I hold on to the faith—the faith I have in Him; faith that He is alive and always with me; faith that I will see Him when my pilgrimage here is done and He calls me home; faith that He will take care of the family that He so lovingly gave me. Now I see that God wanted to *heal* my spiritual being. He wanted to give me *life* beyond the grave and wanted me to know that, in my weakness I will find *His strength.*

In remission, my prayer for the years following is constantly "Lord, if the cancer comes back help me to know that either way I am ok." In other words, whether I'm alive here or alive on the other side, I will be fine. Four years later, another cancer diagnosis came into my life. This time I had to go through a major operation and more chemo. But as hard as it was, I felt His strength in my weakness. I felt His love from my Christian brothers and sisters. I felt the peace He provided to me and my family. I felt the hope through the faith I have in Him, because I knew that either way I would be ok; that was almost four years ago.

Marisol Morales
Calvary Chapel of Philadelphia

Beauty from Ashes

*To console those who mourn in Zion, to give them
beauty for ashes, the oil of joy for mourning,
the garment of praise for the spirit of heaviness;
that they may be called trees of righteousness,
the planting of the LORD, that He may be glorified.*

Isaiah 61:3

Several years ago, I would've described the testimony of my life as a sweet story of the Lord's faithfulness and protection over the granddaughter of a Baptist pastor; saved by the age of six, raised in a Christian home, and graciously blessed with a godly husband and three healthy kids. I was a full-time wife and mom, and loved every minute of all that came along with that calling. Then one day everything changed. From one moment to the next, my life would never be the same again. I was about to walk through an unimaginable test of my faith.

My husband, Dennis, and I were away on a business trip in South Carolina. Dennis told me that he hadn't been feeling well and had developed a really bad cough almost overnight. Despite my reservations, he insisted that we attend his business meeting on Friday night. Throughout the meeting, Dennis couldn't seem to stay awake and kept dozing off with his head in his hand. Knowing that he wasn't feeling well, I finally convinced him to go back to the hotel and get to bed early so we could rest up and make it through the remainder of the weekend. While we were walking out to the car, we said good-bye to some friends and he quickly glanced at me and whispered, "You look beautiful." Then he told me he wasn't feeling well enough to walk up the stairs in the parking garage. Those were the last words Dennis Bair ever spoke to me. As he grabbed my hand to walk towards the door, his body suddenly collapsed; his head slammed against the floor with a thud like I've never heard before. He immediately began to turn blue. A doctor standing nearby started to perform CPR as I stood over my husband's lifeless body. I repeatedly screamed out, "Please don't take him, Lord" as the paramedics lifted him onto the stretcher and rushed us into the ambulance.

As I sat in that small room in the ER awaiting news from the doctor, I somehow knew that life as I had known it was over. Within fifteen minutes, the doctor, accompanied by two nurses, walked into that small room, looked into my eyes and said, "I'm so sorry, Mrs. Bair. We did everything we could do. I'm so sorry, but your husband has died." My husband had died suddenly of a blood clot in his heart that formed as the result of two silent heart attacks he had in the preceding four weeks. I cannot fully describe all that took place in my heart, mind, and body in those minutes, but I can say that it was worse than any nightmare or scene in any movie. Surrounded by all of Dennis' belongings in the hotel room that night, I remember crying out to the Lord like Job had, "The thing I greatly feared has come upon me!" (Job 3:25). I truly felt like my worst nightmare had come to pass. Lying face down on the floor in that hotel room, I cried out to the Lord begging

Him to "please show up and walk me through this or I won't survive!"

The next day I had to fly home and tell my children that their daddy went home to be with Jesus. At that time, Josh was ten, Sammy was seven, and Sarah was six. That moment was one of the darkest moments in my life. In the days and weeks that followed, I remember many, many nights of feeling the agonizing pain of loss and trauma so intense that I would cry out for the Lord to just take me home to heaven. To this day, I cannot fully describe the agony of feeling that throbbing ache in my heart day after day. It felt like a blanket draped over me that I couldn't take off no matter how hard I tried.

Over those dark months, my children watched me endure the unimaginable despair of loss in ways that no child should ever witness. It was during one of those dark days when my son came to me and said, "Mommy, I'm afraid you're going to die, and I can't be an orphan." At that moment, as my son voiced his worst fears to me, the Lord spoke sweetly to my heart that my suffering was not about me. In fact, He laid heavily on my heart that the loss of my precious husband was actually a responsibility that He was entrusting to me, and a road that I must choose to walk by faith, not by sight (see 2 Corinthians 5:7). He revealed to me that this painful journey was my own personal ministry through which I could share in the sufferings of Christ (see 1 Peter 4:13), while at the same time point others to Him who was able to heal their broken hearts and bind up their wounds (see Psalm 147:3).

Right at that moment, I felt as if blinders came off my eyes. By faith, I chose to trust the Lord with His plan and I threw myself into the grieving process. I began pouring out my pain to the Lord in constant prayer, asking Him to use every ounce of it for His glory in my life. Although I personally couldn't envision a hope for my future, I daily chose to believe God's Word that said, " 'For I know the plans I have for you,' declares the LORD, 'plans to prosper you and not to harm you, plans to give you hope and a future' " (Jeremiah 29:11, NIV). On dark days when my faith was weak, I would saturate myself in God's Word and cling to verses that reminded me of His character and faithfulness. As I look back, there were days that my survival seemed moment by moment as I clung to God's Word as daily "food" to strengthen my faith and dependence on Him.

Over time, the Lord began to heal my broken heart and bind up my wounds, just as His Word said He would do for me. I have experienced the Lord's gift of beauty from ashes in my life, and I will never cease to be amazed and captivated by His overwhelming faithfulness and grace. My husband, Dennis, will always be a part of my life and it was an honor to have been his wife. The Lord has since graciously given me the added blessings of another godly husband, Chris, and a fourth child, Leah Grace, who has brought us all so much joy and helped to knit our hearts together as a family. He has truly done "exceedingly abundantly above all" that I could have ever asked or imagined and I will forever stand in awe of His faithful provision in my life! (see Ephesians 3:20). To my God alone be the glory!

Deb (Bair) O'Brien
Calvary Chapel of Philadelphia

Under God's Perfect Care

"For I know the thoughts that I think toward you," says the LORD, "thoughts of peace and not of evil, to give you a future and a hope."

Jeremiah 29:11

The single most influential application of faith came at the very beginning of my salvation and walk with Christ. I had no idea that God in His sovereignty had so much more to show me. I was 29 years old, pregnant, unmarried, living with my boyfriend of seven years, and working in club bands. God in His graciousness had a plan for my life, and led me by faith to a new life. "Therefore, if anyone is in Christ, he is a new creation; old things have passed away; behold, all things have become new" (2 Corinthians 5:17).

Having come out of the 60's and 70's culture, I was living a life based on my autonomous, self-centered, sinful nature—letting it lead the way and have control of my life and decision making. When I received Christ as my savior and made Him Lord of my life, there was so much to be rescued from. The question was, "Where do we begin?" The first Scripture that I memorized and held in my heart as a promise was Romans 8:28. It says, "And we know that all things work together for good to those who love God, to those who are the called according to His purpose."

I had been forgiven so much and was so grateful, but I didn't know how to get myself out of the situation I had gotten myself into. God kept reminding me that I belonged to Him now, and was forgiven; now He would lead the way. Proverbs 3:5-6 says, "Trust in the LORD with all your heart and lean not on your own understanding; in all your ways acknowledge him, and he will make your paths straight" (NIV).

The changes began with a sincere conviction of the Holy Spirit that I had done things my way my whole life; now it was time to yield my will to God's will.

I had counseled with a friend's pastor as to what the Bible said about what I should do. He gave me all the Scriptures; and my job was to obey. I began with my living situation. I needed to address the issue of fornication. But then the question became whether I was to marry the father of my child? He was an unbeliever. It seemed simple, but was certainly painful to sever ties with the man I loved and the father of my unborn child. For the first time I understood that God would lead the way and provide for me. I moved out of his place in Pennsylvania, and found an apartment in New York. I began a new job in New York City, and I watched as God fulfilled His word: "But seek first the kingdom of God and His righteousness, and all these things shall be added to you" (Matthew 6:33).

It was an incredible season of trusting God in the simple and the profound, and watching *all these things* be added to my life.

One night, in the eighth month of my pregnancy, I had no money after paying bills. I was very hungry and worried about my baby for the lack of food I had taken in that week; I prayed. At about 10 o'clock at night there was a knock at my door. There stood a pizza man. I told him through the glass, "I didn't order a pizza." He said that he had been driving around in the rain looking for an address he couldn't find. He asked me if I wanted the pizza. I told him I didn't have any money to pay for it, but he said he wanted me to have it.

God continued to provide for me, even down to the day I had the baby. I was fearful of having to drive myself to the hospital alone, in labor, in New York City traffic. As God in His perfect sovereignty would allow it—I went into labor on a Monday morning (two weeks premature). As I went to the car, I realized there was no traffic at all. It was President's Day 1985, a national holiday. I realized that down to the smallest detail, God cared and was involved.

I began to recognize that God—who had all power to create a universe and rise from the dead—could and would act on my behalf. Every day was a new adventure of faith. In a short six-month period of time, I saw the Lord work and transition me out of a chaotic, confused lifestyle to a sure foundation. "I waited patiently for the LORD; he turned to me and heard my cry. He lifted me out of the slimy pit, out of the mud and mire; he set my feet on a rock and gave me a firm place to stand. He put a new song in my mouth, a hymn of praise to our God. Many will see and fear and put their trust in the LORD" (Psalm 40:1-3, NIV).

At the same time, God had been working on my boyfriend. A fellowship of believers began to pray for me in New York, and for his salvation. About one month later, before our daughter was born, Rob gave his life to Christ. He began to counsel with a godly man that would meet with him weekly to discuss the Bible and disciple him.

From my salvation, and then my boyfriend's, to the birth of our daughter, and then months later our marriage in Christ, to having a family, to serving the Lord together; God indeed had a plan. I felt as though I had literally watched the Red Sea open. He proved to me time and again that He was who He said He was.

"For I am confident of this very thing, that He who began a good work in you will perfect it until the day of Christ Jesus" (Philippians 1:6, NASB).

I thought that our salvation testimony was enough, but in His wisdom, God has allowed us to continue to live by faith.

Heidi Paoletti
Calvary Chapel of Philadelphia

My Rock through the Storm

*The LORD is a refuge for the oppressed,
a stronghold in times of trouble. Those who know
your name will trust in you, for you, LORD,
have never forsaken those who seek you.*

Psalm 9:9-10, NIV

I remember it like it was yesterday. It was late February of 2009; I was in the midst of planning my wedding. The date was set for October of 2009; invitations were sent, and the planning was in high gear. I was taking a shower and felt an unusual lump on my right breast. *What is this?* I thought; *that definitely wasn't there before.* Worry started to settle in and I booked an appointment with my doctor as quickly as possible. Next thing I knew, I was in the middle of a diagnostic mammogram at the age of thirty-four. The doctors and nurses kept reassuring me that it could be nothing. Then I was sent to a surgeon specialist, followed by a very painful needle biopsy. Waiting for the results was agonizing. I kept begging God to not let it be cancer.

A week later, I got the much anticipated phone call, praying for good news. The surgeon said he wanted to see me in his office. *This can't be good,* I thought; so I asked him. When I heard, "It's cancer," my world was shattered. I thought *Why me, God? I thought I was a good Christian. Am I going to die?* I cried and cried until there were no more tears. I didn't understand how this could happen to me at such a young age.

The next couple of weeks were chaotic. They were filled with appointments, tests, and a new world of breast cancer lingo. I had so many difficult decisions to make in such a short period of time. All I wanted was to get this *thing* out of me. I quickly went from asking *Why me?* to *Lord, what's next?*

I was diagnosed with Stage 2B Triple Negative Breast Cancer—the aggressive type that strikes a small percentage of young women with limited treatment options. If detected any later, it would have been too late. It felt like I dodged a bullet. I had a lumpectomy followed by four months of aggressive chemotherapy. In the middle of chemotherapy, I had a genetic test done and it turned out I have the cancer gene BRCA 1 which means I have a very high reoccurrence rate of breast and ovarian cancer. I was scheduled for a full mastectomy after my last chemo treatment on what would have been the week of my wedding. I was numb from the whole experience and kept leaning on God.

Throughout this tragedy, many blessings came into my life. My fiancé and I got married on April 10, 2009 (after being together for ten years), three days before I started chemotherapy. I received so much love and support from my church family at Calvary, and from my loved ones at home. I became closer to our Lord. Throughout it all, He kept telling me He would be with me. "And the LORD, He is the One who goes before you. He will be with you, He will not leave you nor forsake you; do not fear nor be dismayed" (Deuteronomy 31:8).

As I reflect on my journey today, I didn't understand then why I went through cancer. I hung onto this verse, "For I know the plans I have for you," declares the LORD, "plans to prosper you and not to harm you, plans to give you hope and a future" (Jeremiah 29:11, NIV). I had faith our Lord was in control of my life.

In 2010 and 2011, two of my closest aunts were struck with colon and breast cancer, respectively. I was the first person they contacted to answer their questions. I was more than happy to support them in any way I could. If it wasn't for my cancer diagnosis, I wouldn't know how to comfort and encourage them. My cancer experience became very clear to me, and it humbled me. This verse hit home for me:

"Praise be to the God and Father of our Lord Jesus Christ, the Father of compassion and the God of all comfort, who comforts us in all our troubles, so that we can comfort those in any trouble with the comfort we ourselves have received from God" (2 Corinthians 1:3-4, NIV).

Today I am at a better place. Before cancer, I was miserable at a corporate job working forty-five to sixty hours a week, with a long commute. I had no direction, nor sense of purpose. Cancer forced me to slow down and reevaluate my priorities in life. I am serving our Lord in the Women's Ministry encouraging other cancer survivors; I am working from home, loving what I do by helping women, and I have a different perspective on life.

The most important lesson I have learned is to have faith during the difficult times; having faith not only in the big things in life, but also in the little things. I have faith in our Lord Jesus Christ who will "never leave you nor forsake you" (Hebrews 13:5b). I have faith that our eternal home is in heaven. Amen.

Tracy (Chan) Rios
Calvary Chapel of Philadelphia

CALL TO ME

Call to Me, and I will answer you, and show you great and mighty things, which you do not know.

Jeremiah 33:3

My mom is well-known for her concern and prayer for the hippies. In the late 1960's and early 1970's, a counter-culture movement swept the world. Young people from ages ten to those in adulthood, who considered themselves young, began to search for deeper meaning to life. This quest led to experimentation with drugs, alternative lifestyles, and sexual experimentation. Though the movement claimed to be all about peace and love, it was marked by the destruction of lives.

During those harrowing times, it was not unusual to see droves of young people strung out on drugs roaming the streets or sleeping in parks. Hippies were distinguishable by their long hair, faded jeans, ragged garments, and more often than not by their lack of personal hygiene.

Mom, seeing the disheveled members of this movement, began to pray with a fury. Next door to our house, a dear friend, Kay Matteson, had a prayer meeting on Thursday mornings. Mom soon turned the whole prayer meeting into one impassioned voice interceding for a lost generation.

One day a young man named Lonnie Frisbee was brought to our home. He was short, bearded, and wore the garments of a bona fide hippie. However, Lonnie was distinct from his generation. Lonnie was born-again. Mom was enthralled. She sat down with Lonnie and began to pepper him with questions. She wanted to know what first drew him to the hippie lifestyle. She wanted to know how he came to know Jesus. Lonnie answered Mom's questions while Mom listened with rapt attention. A deep friendship formed. Soon Lonnie and his young wife, Connie, were regularly attending Calvary Chapel Costa Mesa.

Lonnie began to grow spiritually under the Bible teaching. He had an amazing gift of evangelism. Lonnie understood the quest, hunger, and disillusionment of his generation. He began to lead his peers to Jesus and then to Calvary Chapel. The church began to boil over with hippies who had finally found the answer to their quest in Jesus.

It wasn't long before the parents of the hippies, curious about the radical change in their children, came to Calvary Chapel. Many of the parents attending came under the influence of the Spirit and were born-again as well.

Mom's work was not over, in fact, it had only begun. As she continued to attend and lead the prayer meetings next door, she also began to minister to the young believers that were coming to church. Mom was always alert and looking for anyone who appeared to be in need: a young girl crying, a bewildered look, someone sitting alone. She approached the one in need and engaged them in conversation. Soon Mom would be ministering and praying with them.

Often when I came home from school, I would find Mom outside, her Bible open on her lap, deep in conversation with a young man or woman. She was always available to listen, really listen, and pray with anyone who had a need.

Mom was the camp-nurse at our first all church retreat. Her only experience with nursing was raising four children and that her mother had been a nurse. Mom bandaged wounds, administered medicine, prayed, listened, and dispensed Scriptures with enthusiasm and joy.

Sometime later a need arose for these young female believers to be taught "good things" by an older Christian woman. Mom was asked to teach a Bible study to these women. She was both excited and apprehensive. She poured over her Bible, made copious notes, read commentaries, and practiced her whole message several times into my brother's tape recorder before she taught her first study.

God was with mom. He anointed her, spoke through her, and, as usual, ministered His love and grace through her. The Bible study grew and grew until it had to be held in the main sanctuary of Calvary Chapel.

Mom's whole ministry to women began with a passion for a lost generation. She set herself to pray when she saw the gaping need in these young people for Jesus. God met and answered Mom in a mighty way!

Faith often has its beginning in need or deficit. When we, like my mother, pray and seek God over the need, faith has its great initiation. God begins to work in amazing ways.

Mom was not only a part of praying for the hippies, but God allowed her to be a participant in the answer to her prayers!

Kay Smith
As told by her daughter, Cheryl Brodersen
Calvary Chapel of Costa Mesa
Santa Ana, California

Pray and Believe

*Therefore I say to you,
whatever things you ask when you pray,
believe that you receive them, and you will have them.*

Mark 11:24

Mom clung to the practice of praying about everything. Once Mom committed something to Jesus, she was sure He was going to work. This principle was often tested and proved in her life.

Mom loved to pray. It didn't matter the occasion, she always found an excuse to pray. Whether it was over a parking place, a family squabble, a national tragedy, or a pressing need, Mom prayed. Mom prayed while she was driving, cooking, cleaning, walking, or exercising.

I remember many days coming home from school hearing Mom on the phone praying with someone. The sound was both inspiring and comforting.

On one occasion, Mom was driving with three of her dearest friends. Her friends had accompanied her to a speaking engagement. When Mom was finished, the four women had lunch together and then headed home in the car. Mom was driving and got a little carried away with the fellowship and joy of the moment. Her foot rested a little too heavily on the gas pedal. Looking in the rear-view mirror,

Mom saw blue and red lights flashing. "Pray girls!" she quickly responded. The women all bowed their heads and began praying immediately.

Mom also said a quick prayer before rolling down the window and addressing the officer.

The policeman peered inside the car. "Lady, do you realize how fast you were going?"

Mom smiled at the officer. "I'm afraid I don't. I am so sorry. I think I got carried away. I was having such a wonderful time with my friends; I wasn't concentrating on my driving like I should have been."

Again the officer looked deep inside the vehicle. "I really should give you a ticket, but I see that your friends are all praying for you, so I am going to let you off this time."

The friends, who had been interceding for Mom, opened their eyes and the whole car began to profusely thank the officer for his mercy.

Gesturing at Mom, the officer extracted a promise from Mom's friends, "Do you girls promise to keep your friend to the speed limit?"

Enthusiastically they all agreed to help Mom watch her speed. The officer turned to go, but before he dismissed them he said, "Perhaps you could all pray for me now."

"Yes!" they all chorused. Betty, who was sitting in the backseat, wrote his name down. The rest of the ride was interspersed with thanksgiving for God's mercy and prayer for the merciful policeman.

Mom's faith in God was built as she watched God answer one prayer after another in amazing ways!

Kay Smith
As told by her daughter, Cheryl Brodersen
Calvary Chapel of Costa Mesa
Santa Ana, California

Jesus Never Fails

The LORD is righteous in her midst, He will do no unrighteousness. Every morning He brings His justice to light; He never fails.

Zephaniah 3:5

As I dried the plate in my hand I looked over at my dad who was washing the dishes. "Dad," I asked. "Were you ever concerned that your father would never be healed?"

Dad paused for a moment, his hands elbow-deep in the suds. "No, never."

"Never?" I shot back rather incredulously. "How can that be? Wasn't grandma worried?"

Again dad paused. He looked out the kitchen window as if retrieving the whole scene in his mind. I loved these times when dad recounted the faith-building moments of his childhood.

"My mom, your grandma, never worried. She set the tone for the whole family. I remember asking her once about my dad. She smiled at me and said, 'Chuck, Jesus never fails. You will see.' From that moment on, I knew Jesus was going to do something."

My questions centered on the time when my grandfather, my dad's dad, had a nervous breakdown. My father was only fifteen at the time. Both he and my grandmother were forced out into the workforce to try to support the family while they waited for my grandfather to recover.

"What was grandpa like during this time?"

"He was bed-ridden and unable to communicate. He was in an almost catatonic state. He seemed unaware of his environment. He rarely moved. The family took turns feeding him and attending to his needs."

"How did he get better?"

"As you know, my mother loved to have company over for Sunday dinner after church. On one of those Sundays, an Indian prince, who had shared that morning at our church, came over for dinner. He was a colorful guy and had an amazing testimony. A year later, after my dad's nervous breakdown, Prince Marthondon showed up at our front door, his big white Cadillac parked out on the street. He told my mother that he was driving through Ventura when the Lord told him to go to Brother Smith's house and pray for him. My mom ushered him through the house to grandpa's bed. Prince Marthondon placed his hands on my dad and said, 'Brother Smith, be healed in the name of the Lord Jesus Christ.' Instantly my dad responded by looking up at the prince and smiling, 'Well Prince Marthondon, how are you doing? Great to see you!' My dad was completely healed from that moment on. He went back to work a few days later."

"That was it?"

"That was it. It was instant and miraculous. We, my brothers, sister and I were all in the room and watched in amazement. My mom was the only one in the room that didn't seem surprised. She looked at all of us and smiling declared, 'Jesus never fails!'"

I have often thought about what it must have been like for my grandma, living during those depression years, with four children, and an ailing husband to attend to. Though life must have been so difficult, her faith in Jesus was unshakable. On her gravestone is the motto that she believed, shared, instilled, and clung to, JESUS NEVER FAILS!

Maude Smith (Mother of Pastor Chuck Smith)
As told by her granddaughter, Cheryl Brodersen
Calvary Chapel of Costa Mesa
Santa Ana, California

Walk by Faith and Not by Feelings

*But I am like a green olive tree in the house of God;
I trust in the mercy of God forever and ever. I will praise
You forever, because You have done it; and in the presence
of Your saints I will wait on Your name, for it is good.*

Psalm 52:8-9

I had just graduated from Bible College convinced that God had a plan for my life, and that I wanted to serve Him wherever or however He wanted. I was holding onto Jeremiah 29:11. It says, "'For I know the thoughts that I think toward you,' says the LORD, 'thoughts of peace and not of evil, to give you a future and a hope.'" I was truly beginning to understand that when I made choices or plans apart from seeking God, I fell flat on my face and messed up big time. He was showing me that "I am crucified with Christ: nevertheless I live; yet not I, but Christ liveth in me: and the life which I now live in the flesh I live by the faith of the Son of God, who loved me, and gave himself for me" (Galatians 2:20, KJV). Shortly after I graduated, my faith was going to be challenged and tested as so often happens when we make a choice to follow God with our whole hearts.

My husband and I met in Bible College. When we met, I had no idea that he would eventually become my husband. We were close friends in school, and I grew to respect him and value his friendship. After we both graduated, we continued our friendship, but that's all it was—friendship. Then one day, God was speaking to my heart and told me that Trevor was going to be my husband. I have to say, my first response was, "Um, I don't think so; he's my best friend. He's like the brother I never had." God continued to work on my heart, showing me His plan and asking me to trust and obey Him. I spent a lot of time reading the Word and in prayer. Philippians 4:6-7 became real to me. It says, "Be anxious for nothing, but in everything by prayer and supplication, with thanksgiving, let your requests be made known to God; and the peace of God, which surpasses all understanding, will guard your hearts and minds through Christ Jesus." God also reminded me that I had committed my life, and all rights regarding it, to Him. "For you died, and your life is hidden with Christ in God." (Colossians 3:3).

I knew that I was at a crossroads; God was laying out His plan and calling on my life before me. I could either obey Him, even though I was afraid and didn't understand, or I could go my own way and miss what He had planned for me. It was very clear to me that I could choose to walk by faith (believing in what I could not see), or by my feelings (believing in what I could see). By His grace alone, I chose to trust my Father. Even though I was afraid and confused, I took that first step of obedience and faith, and said *yes* to God. And as He always does, God took care of the rest.

We got engaged soon after; we have been married now for almost 13 years, and we have been blessed with three children. I never could have chosen a more perfect husband.

I thank God daily for giving me the most amazing, humble, Spirit-filled man I have ever met. I would have missed the biggest gift and blessing in my life if I had listened to my fear and my feelings rather than listening to God asking me to trust Him. I cannot tell you what a huge lesson I learned, and how often I go back to that situation where God taught me the importance and the necessity of trusting Him even when I cannot see or understand. He reminds me so often to walk by faith and not by my feelings. I still don't have this down completely, but thankfully, I can fall back on His promise that, "If we are faithless, He remains faithful; He cannot deny Himself" (2 Timothy 2:13).

Right after we got married, God called us to move to the inner city of Philadelphia, to one of the worst areas of the city, to minister in His name. We needed to step out in faith and trust Him every day living in the midst of some very difficult circumstances. I believe that God supernaturally protected us and sustained us the entire three and a half years that we lived there. Looking back, those were some of the hardest years; yet they were some of the most precious years. Those were years of major faith building, growing, and testing, as well as preparation for the years to come. Everything that I had depended on in the past was taken away; I *had* to trust the Lord. Not only did I need to learn how to be a wife, I was in a new and very unfamiliar place that was certainly out of my comfort zone. I remember as I would drive back home into our neighborhood, I could sense the darkness and oppression; it was almost tangible. Yet God was with us, and we knew that He had us there for a reason. It was amazing, and at the same time it was so hard; I cried often during that season. I praise Him for allowing us the privilege of ministering to some really awesome kids who lived there (they will always have a special place in my heart), as well as ministering with some of the most incredible servants of Christ. In His grace, we learned and grew while being broken on an almost daily basis for the people of that neighborhood. I realize now that God allowed the testing of my faith in regards to marrying my husband to allow me to trust Him in this next season. As God showed Himself faithful on my behalf, it allowed me to trust Him for that next step of faith. That was the beginning of our life together, and as each year goes by, He shows me more and more that living by faith is the only way to truly live.

Kristin Steenbakkers
Calvary Chapel of Philadelphia

Faith's Expectation

You, O God, sent a plentiful rain, Whereby You confirmed Your inheritance, when it was weary.

Psalm 68:9

"Why is it so hot," I whined as I brushed the flies off my face and shielded my eyes from the dust. It was a scorching day as we rattled down the dirt road on our way to Pachera, Mexico. Due to the lack of air conditioning in those days, all the windows were rolled down in our carryall truck as all eight of us kids were piled in the back. My mother would play Bible trivia games she invented to keep us distracted from the blazing heat and the tedious journey. Normally this was the rainy season, where we were greeted with blooming crops and lush corn; though this year the rains had not come and the fields were empty. What a concerning problem this was, my father had said, for it was the only livelihood these Mexican families had.

We arrived at our destination and unloaded the trailer while Mom proceeded to make us lunch. I still remember clearly sitting around the old fold-out table as we ate our sardine and cracker sandwiches. Halfway through we heard a rapid knock at the front door, and my older brother was elected to answer. It wasn't long before he came back with a report, "It is a man with a bunch of papers in his hand. He wants to talk to you, Dad." We children continued eating our modest lunch as we curiously waited to find out what the man wanted. Soon Dad returned, deep in thought and with a concerned look on his face. He then declared, "We need to pray!" and went on to explain why.

It was the town mayor who had come with a petition to throw us out of town. Apparently, the Catholic priest had told all the villagers that the cause for the drought was that the "Christian missionaries" were coming and evangelizing, causing an evil omen. My dad then politely, but firmly, explained to the mayor that we were not the cause of the rain's absence because our God was a good God. He then told him that he was going to ask God to send rain from heaven, and that if it did not rain by this time tomorrow we would leave. The Mayor seemed satisfied with this answer and quickly departed.

My dad loved situations that left us with no recourse but to trust in our Heavenly Father's resources alone—and this was one of those times. "Now we need to ask the Lord to bring the rain," Dad announced as we all got on our knees and he led us in prayer. Being the youngest of eight, I don't remember the prayers, but I do remember Dad excitedly patting me on the back and saying, "Praise the Lord! Let's see what He will do!"

It wasn't twenty-four hours later—not even twelve hours later—but by that afternoon the sky was blanketed with so many thunderclouds that the whole town was dark…and it began to rain. Sheets of rain fell fast and furiously, saturating the entire countryside. It rained so hard that the streets turned into rivers and the people were forced to put bags of sand in front of their doorsteps to keep the water from seeping in. There was such intensity that the sod roof on the Catholic Church collapsed!

Our God had spoken! He had authenticated His work and confirmed His inheritance as only He can. Now Pachera is known as the town of the "Cristianos" (in English, the Christians), and those signatures that were on the petition to ban us from that town are the same names of many saints who have since believed in the faithful God of the Evangelical Missionaries.

> *"...prove me now herewith, saith the LORD of hosts, if I will not open you the windows of heaven, and pour you out a blessing, that there shall not be room enough to receive it"* (Malachi 3:10, KJV).

Today I am serving with my husband and children as a missionary in York, England. No, we do not have to pray for rain in England, but the testing of our faith never ceases as the spiritual battles remain the same. How thankful I am for the heritage I was given as a child to see how big my God is, and to expectantly live in the reality of His faithfulness from day to day. William Carey said, *"Expect great things from God, attempt great things for God."* May we never stop expecting to see goodness from our Father's hand in the land of the living. "I would have lost heart, unless I had believed that I would see the goodness of the LORD in the land of the living" (Psalm 27:13).

Nancy Sylvester
Calvary Chapel York
York, England

Forever Faithful

He who calls you is faithful, who also will do it.
1 Thessalonians 5:24

After many years of rebellion, I surrendered my life to Jesus at 18 years of age, finally recognizing that nothing else could truly satisfy me. I was excited about my new faith; I enrolled in Bible College, and just wanted to seek His face and follow Him all my days. During my junior year of college, I met Kirk. We instantly hit it off. We had many similar interests, but more importantly, a desire to sincerely follow the Lord and serve His Body.

We were married in November of 1994, and had our first child, a daughter, nearly two years later. Around our daughter's first birthday, we found out we were expecting Baby #2. Meanwhile, Kirk began experiencing headaches. After several doctor visits, and attempts to treat what was thought to be migraines and allergies, the doctor ordered a CT scan. To our absolute shock, the CT scan revealed a destructive growth in Kirk's sinuses. An appointment was set up to see a specialist, and a biopsy was performed a few days later. The diagnosis was sinus cancer, which had already invaded the brain and lymph nodes. The prognosis was not good; however, we all agreed to try all treatments that were available to us. Aggressive chemotherapy and radiation began soon afterward. Within a few weeks, Kirk began to experience the negative side effects, like fatigue and nausea. He also developed second and third degree burns on his head and neck from the radiation. Through this time, we were upheld by the Lord Himself, and the prayers and support of His saints.

After about four months of treatments, the doctors felt optimistic that the cancerous tumor had been destroyed. A few weeks later, I gave birth to a baby boy, extremely grateful to the Lord that Kirk was there for his birth. We really tried to get back to a normal life after the whirlwind we had just experienced. However, there were still frequent doctor visits, regular MRIs and CT scans, and many hospitalizations for various complications that arose. But still, we were thankful that God had sustained Kirk's life to this point, and were soberly aware that things could change at any time.

About three years after his initial diagnosis, a scheduled scan revealed a new tumor in his brain. Surgeries, hospitalizations, complications, more chemo and radiation took place for nearly two more years, but eventually the cancer and aggressive treatments began to take its toll. He lost a lot of weight, and his physical strength and cognitive functioning began to deteriorate. I took him to the hospital one October day for a scheduled infusion of chemo. When the doctor saw him, she told me he was dying, and that I should take him home. Although this didn't come as a surprise to me, it was probably the most difficult part of that journey, because Kirk and I had gone through this nearly 5-year-trial *together*, and had come to accept that this was what God had called us to. Over these years, we grew to love and appreciate each other more, and also grew in our faith and trust in the Lord. We even laughed at some of the craziness of it all, and were humbled by the many open doors God gave us to share about His sustaining grace. But this journey had now come to the point where I had to make the decision to stop all efforts to fight this cancer. I had to trust that God would be the Good Shepherd who would walk my husband through the valley of the shadow of death, and take him safely home to heaven. I had done everything that I could—medically, physically and spiritually.

I brought him home with hospice care. He was a courageous and gentle patient, submissive to God's sovereignty and plan for his life. Even though he could no longer walk, see, or hear, when he was able to speak, it was a word about Jesus and His goodness, or he would sing a few lines from a worship song.

The Lord woke me up early on the morning of November 23, 2002. Kirk's breathing became shallow, and I crawled into his hospital bed. I held his head in my hands as he took his last breath. I immediately felt despair as I had never known, then within a few minutes, the Lord opened me up to John 14:27. He spoke to my heart, "although I took Kirk, this is what I leave with you… 'Peace I leave with you, My peace I give to you; not as the world gives do I give you. Let not your heart be troubled, neither let it be afraid.'" I looked out the window, the sky was blue and the sun was shining. My sorrow turned to joy because I was so happy for Kirk, that he was with the Lord, and he had run his race well, and more importantly, finished well. I almost sighed in relief, feeling as if we had been victorious in the trial of our lives—and it was over.

I assumed life would now find some kind of normal for the kids and me. Yet, I had no idea what grief was, but soon learned; it came as waves without warning with sleepless nights, restless days and many tears. But as time went on, through the comfort of the Holy Spirit and the support from family and friends, the sting began to subside and God gave me the grace to accept what happened. I think often of Ecclesiastes 7:3, "Sorrow is better than laughter, for by a sad countenance the heart is made better." I'm thankful to God for the open doors this experience has continually given me to encourage those who have suffered loss, especially widows. He has shown me that reaching out to others, especially when I don't feel like it, will bring healing to my own heart.

God has given to each of us a measure of faith (see Romans 12:3). Some also attribute faith to their upbringing, cultural background, birth order, education, past experience, etc.; these all can contribute to our faith. As I think of the role faith had and continues to have in my life, I can only speak of His faithfulness. There have been times when my faith was very weak. As I encountered the hardships that come with being a single parent, I questioned the Lord as to whether this was really His best plan for my kids and me. It is at those times, when I am without much faith, that He has remained faithful to me, for He cannot deny Himself (see 2 Timothy 2:13). How could we have faith in One who wasn't faithful? *Faithfulness*[1] is defined as "true to one's word, promises or vows; steady in allegiance or affection; loyal, constant, reliable, trusted, believed"...and it's the essence of who He is. Sarah, Abraham's wife, had faith to conceive, because she judged Him faithful who had promised (see Hebrews 11:11). Asaph wrote, "With my mouth will I make known Your faithfulness to all generations" (Psalm 89:1). David wrote, "Your faithfulness endures to all generations" (Psalm 119:90). As we read about the saints throughout the Scriptures proclaiming His faithfulness, we can be assured that He will be faithful to us, to our children, and the generations to follow. His faithfulness will not stop with our generation. He is the same yesterday, today and forever. Even as sin, iniquity and hardship abound, we can't allow these things to define our faith, or our God. The times where we may, He will remain faithful. He is able to keep that which we have committed to Him until that Day (see 2 Timothy 1:12), and to hold our faith and keep us in Him because He is faithful. He always has been; He always will be. "He who calls you is faithful, who also will do it" (1 Thessalonians 5:24).

Mary Thompson
Calvary Chapel of Philadelphia

---

1. *Faithfulness:* Dictionary.com. Unabridged. Random House, Inc. 26 Mar. 2012. <Dictionary.com http://dictionary.reference.com/browse/faithfulness>.

A Walk of Faith Testimony

Now the LORD had said unto Abram, Get thee out of thy country, and from thy kindred, and from thy father's house, unto a land that I will shew thee:

Genesis 12:1, KJV

When we exercise faith, do we sometimes even realize we are exercising faith? I think of the woman who pushed through the crowd to touch the hem of Jesus' garment. Was she thinking, "I have to exercise faith right now and do this" or was she just doing it because she had a need and knew that Jesus could meet that need? She found herself in a difficult circumstance considering all she had gone through trying to get healed. Now the only thing left for her to do was to push through the crowd to touch the hem of His garment.

So when we step out in faith, do we really know that we are stepping out in faith?

I remember many years ago, taking steps of faith that would take us from the home we had built on 82 Abbey Road in Nottingham to a house in Shaftesbury, in the South of England. We had not even seen this house, and didn't know the area to which we would be moving.

It didn't seem like a step of faith at the time. It seemed like it was what needed to be done; that was the situation we found ourselves facing. I remember everything we owned was in the moving van outside; we were sleeping on the mattress on the floor, and our three children were doing the same.

As we lay there, my husband, Malcolm, started to get all melancholy on me. He was reminiscing about having our third child born in that very room.

I felt like we were on an exciting journey that was taking us to a place I had never been before. The next morning as the van driver began putting the last things into his van he asked us about the place we were going. It was a surprise to him that all we had were directions on how to get there. "Never seen it?" he said, "So, this is a faith house?" I guess you could call it that; although we had never looked at it like that.

When we pulled up at our "faith house," the driver was jumping around praising the Lord and shouting hallelujah. He said, "I have been holding my breath for the four hours it took us to get here because I have driven quite a few families to faith houses, and I have never seen one as beautiful as this!"

And it was a beautiful house in a beautiful place—one of the most picturesque places in England. We were there for only six short months, and we once again found ourselves moving from Shaftesbury, England to Santa Ana, California. Once again we moved to a house we had never seen.

Maranatha Music had arranged for someone Malcolm would be working with to find us a home. Malcolm was working as a pastor to some musicians from Calvary Chapel Costa Mesa. This home was once again a place of "faith."

Some looking on said, "Wow, that's a big step of faith." It didn't seem like a step of faith. At that time it was something that was set before us and it was the next thing to do.

Then after seven and a half years, we moved from California to Merritt Island, Florida, to Cornerstone (which is now Calvary Chapel). Again we moved into a place we had never seen, having no idea what it looked like.

With all those uncertainties, people may have said, "My, you're taking a great step of faith," but I didn't look at it like that. It just seemed like it was the next step in following the Lord's leading for our family.

The wonderful thing about all this was after we had lived in our rental home for two years, the Lord wonderfully blessed me by allowing me to build a home that I was able to have a hand in designing! It was a wonderful home in which to raise our three children. This home was a gift to me, because I never would have asked for anything like it. Talk about a faith house!

So, when we exercise faith, do we even realize we are exercising faith? No! For me it was more a matter of knowing my God, trusting Him and following His lead just one step—or one house—at a time.

Carol Wild
Calvary Chapel Merritt Island
Merritt Island, Florida

My Journey of Faith

*That the trial of your faith, being much more
precious than of gold that perisheth,
though it be tried with fire, might be found unto praise and
honour and glory at the appearing of Jesus Christ.*

1 Peter 1:7, KJV

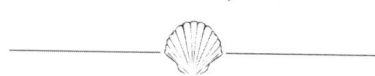

My journey of faith began when I was born to a *real* woman of faith, my mother. She made a giant impact on my life as a believer. My mother's parents were not believers and her father was an alcoholic, but somehow all four of their daughters became strong believers. A lady witnessed to one daughter who accepted the Lord and then she witnessed to her sisters and took them to church. The first sister became a single missionary in Africa for 36 years. One daughter raised two missionary sons who served on two continents. Through the witness of this one lady, people on four continents were reached with the gospel. It is amazing to me the way God draws people to Himself even when there are no other believers in their family.

My mother lost a baby son at the age of one to diphtheria, and also another son who drowned at the age of nine. I remember the women of the church coming over to console my mom when her son drowned, but it was my mother who consoled them. I never heard her get angry or question God. She always said that she was grateful for the time God gave her with these sweet boys and that for some reason God wanted her precious red-headed boys with Him. She also said there were worse places you could have two boys waiting for you. She knew they were with their Lord waiting to see her again one day.

One of my teenage friends asked me if I was saved and I told him that I wasn't because I could never be as *good* as my mother. Little did I know at the time that it wasn't that she was good, but that God was good, and she trusted Him with the very lives of her family. He was the one who strengthened her during the bad times. My mother had an "eternal view" of life. She knew that she was only a small part of a very big plan that God had—and that plan included eternity.

I was married at the age of nineteen. It was not long into the marriage that I realized my husband was an alcoholic. I became pregnant at the age of twenty but lost the baby in the fifth month. I was devastated and not walking with the Lord. I drank my way through this terrible time in my life unlike my mother who fully trusted God with the loss of her children. Thankfully, I know my mother was always faithfully praying for her children. The following year, my sister told me she had asked the Lord to come into her life and she didn't want to go to heaven and leave me behind. Well, I never went anywhere alone, and I was especially close to my sister; I didn't want to be left behind, so I accepted the Lord also. Only God knows for sure the exact date I got "saved." I went forward at church many times as a child to receive Christ, but it became real to me in my twenties. It was at this time that I began to understand "trusting the Lord" and the "eternal view."

I was twenty-two years old when my daughter was born. Then I suffered another miscarriage two years later. Unlike the first loss, I had perfect peace about the loss of this baby, knowing that God was in control and that He doesn't make any mistakes. "For I know the plans I have for you," declares the LORD, "plans to prosper you and not to harm you, plans to give you hope and a future" (Jeremiah 29:11, NIV). I knew I would see these children in heaven someday. My son was born when I was twenty-nine and the marriage continued to deteriorate even further.

We had been attending a church that was going through some very difficult times. I would come home from church with my stomach tied in knots from all the fighting and disunity. My unsaved husband told me I should start attending another church in the area. My human-nature yelled, *Who does he think he is? He doesn't even go to church and he is going to tell me where to attend? NO WAY!* Of course, God quieted me down and said, *I can lead you through this unsaved husband of yours.* So I began attending the church he recommended. Shortly thereafter this church hired me. God knew that after I started working for the church my husband would leave us for five and a half years, and we would need the support of the church and staff. It was all in "His plan"!

During this time, I was completely dependent on the Lord both financially and emotionally. We were never well-off but the Lord did supply all our needs. It was a hard time, but a time when I was closest to the Lord. I saw the Lord work in some amazing ways.

My husband lost everything he had and turned to the Lord. He went to a Christian rehab for seven months and accepted the Lord. He then returned to our family. The next two years were amazing. We went to home fellowships and church every week. It was great having a Christian marriage. Then the unthinkable happened; he fell off the roof and broke his heel. The doctor gave him pain medicine which started his addiction up again—worse than ever. For the past sixteen years he has had his ups and downs, but still struggles with his addiction. I have learned that God is still in control and He has a plan.

Then, in October of 2010, I was having trouble with indigestion and went to see the doctor. After many tests, I was diagnosed with pancreatic cancer. It was caught early and I was told that the doctors would do a Whipple procedure which would remove the head of the pancreas, part of the small bowel, and possibly part of the stomach. I went into surgery on December 17, 2010. When I woke from surgery, everyone was looking at each other asking who was going to tell me something. I knew it had to be bad. Finally, my daughter told me they could not operate because the cancer had grown on the hepatic artery. I knew that was a death sentence. It's funny though, because it was as if someone just said they were going to the store. I had been living with an "eternal view" for so long and had seen God work in my life in so many ways that I knew God was still in control. Death meant going to heaven to be with Him and my family and friends that went on before me. I've been looking forward to heaven for a long time.

I asked God that this would not be in vain but would be an opportunity to use it for His honor and glory. He has given me so many opportunities to tell the doctors and caregivers about the Lord. It is exciting to see Him bring people into my life both to witness to, and to encourage and support me. The journey can be a hard one. There are so many decisions to be made about treatments and going out on disability. There is the big unknown: *when and how will God take you. Will it be painful?* These are the things that bring me back to faith. Has God ever let me down? No! Has He ever left me alone? No! Had He ever made plans to harm me? No! Will He be with me? Yes! Will He give me strength for all this? Yes! I pray that He will get the honor and glory through all of this.

God performs miracles even today. But when He leaves the addictions, the illnesses and doesn't perform the miracle, is He still in control? Yes! He is performing His good work. Through these life situations, God uses us to tell the good news to others, and to show them that He is faithful to get us through these tough times. I really do look forward to the day Jesus will come for me and I will finally be home.

"Praise be to the God and Father of our Lord Jesus Christ! In his great mercy he has given us new birth into a living hope through the resurrection of Jesus Christ from the dead, and into an inheritance that can never perish, spoil or fade—kept in heaven for you, who through faith are shielded by God's power…In this you greatly rejoice" (1 Peter 1:3-6, NIV).

Evelyn Yerkes
Calvary Chapel of Philadelphia

Embrace the Race

Run with patience the race that is set before us.
Hebrews 12:1, KJV

"Have you been doing self-exams?" the gynecologist asked me. "No," I answered a bit hesitantly. I quickly added that I really didn't know how to do that. At 37 years of age, I'd only been to the gynecologist a few times prior to this visit. I saw the concern on her face. "Feel this," she said, guiding my hand to feel a lump under my left arm pit.

I had just returned from a mission trip to Mexico with a team from Calvary Chapel Philly. I was quite elated at all the Lord had taught me, and how He had allowed me to serve Him during this amazing trip. In the "blink of an eye" my world as I knew it changed dramatically! I had been a Christian for a few years, and I began to pray quickly and quietly. I knew that the Lord was impressing on my mind to schedule further appointments for the scans that the doctor had suggested. The results were immediate—it was a tumor, most likely cancerous. When my husband returned home from a business trip, we went to see a surgeon, at my gynecologist's advice. A needle biopsy confirmed that it was cancer. For the first time in my "Christian life" I became completely dependent on the Lord. *Why now? Why at such a young age?* It seemed at the time like a death sentence. I had never sought the Lord for a verse before. I began to ask the Lord to direct my thoughts, words, and actions. The Holy Spirit was so faithful to give me a number of verses. As my husband, Bob, and I looked ahead, although not too far—more like a day at a time—the Lord gave me Ecclesiastes 3:1: "To everything there is a season, and a time to every purpose under heaven" (KJV). He also gave me this verse: "I am with you always, even to the end of the age" (Matthew 28:20).

I found that the Lord taught me to pray over every aspect of my care. I had such a peace about those involved in my care. Psalm 16:7-8 says that "I will praise the Lord, who counsels me; even at night my heart instructs me. I have set the Lord always before me. Because he is at my right hand, I will not be shaken" (NIV).

Psalm 55:17 says, "Evening and morning and at noon I will pray, and cry aloud, and He shall hear my voice." Following surgery to remove the tumor, I needed to decide on a course of treatment. Bob and I listened intently to all that was told to us. It's amazing how the Lord led us through every aspect of care. I totally learned to trust in Jesus. Proverbs 3:5-6 says, "Trust in the Lord with all your heart and lean not on your own understanding; in all your ways acknowledge him, and he will make your path straight" (NIV).

I needed to have radiation and chemotherapy. At this time, the Lord gave me a verse that I will carry with me until He takes me home: "Run with patience the race that is set before us" (Hebrews 12:1c, KJV). That is what He had me do. I *ran* with 40 doses of radiation and then went right into chemotherapy. I chose the strongest "chemo cocktail" available. The side effects were not paramount on my mind. After losing my hair, running a fever high enough to spend a week in the hospital, giving myself shots of a medication to raise my too-low white count, needing to be double-dosed with chemo; I completed my treatments.

I've been cancer free for 18 years now. The "side-effect" that I will always have is the knowledge that Jesus "...restored me to health and let me live" (Isaiah 38:16, NIV). May I use all that He taught me to encourage others.

Pat Zaborowski
Calvary Chapel of Philadelphia

*Blessed be the God and Father of our Lord Jesus Christ, who according to His abundant mercy has begotten us again to a living hope through the resurrection of Jesus Christ from the dead, to an inheritance incorruptible and undefiled and that does not fade away, reserved in heaven for you, who are kept by the power of God through **faith** for salvation ready to be revealed in the last time.*

*In this you greatly rejoice, though now for a little while, if need be, you have been grieved by various trials, that the genuineness of your **faith**, being much more precious than gold that perishes, though it is tested by fire, may be found to praise, honor, and glory at the revelation of Jesus Christ, whom having not seen you love. Though now you do not see Him, yet believing, you rejoice with joy inexpressible and full of glory, receiving the end of your **faith**—the salvation of your souls.*

1 Peter 1:3-9